3-INGREDIENT
SLOW COOKER
COMFORT FOODS

3-INGREDIENT
SLOW COOKER
COMFORT FOODS

200 Recipes for Flavorful Favorites, Slow-Cooker Style!

Robert Hildebrand and Carol Hildebrand

FAIR WINDS
PRESS
GLOUCESTER, MASSACHUSETTS

First published in the USA in 2006 by

Fair Winds Press, a member of

Quayside Publishing Group

33 Commercial Street

Gloucester, MA 01930

10 09 08 07 06   1 2 3 4 5

ISBN-13: 978-1-59233-251-9
ISBN-10: 1-59233-251-X

Library of Congress Cataloging-in-Publication Data
Hildebrand, Carol.
  3-ingredient slow cooker comfort foods : 200 recipes for flavorful favorites slow
cooker style! / Carol Hildebrand and Robert Hildebrand.
      p. cm.
   Includes index.
   ISBN-13: 978-1-59233-251-9
   ISBN-10: 1-59233-251-X
1. Electric cookery, Slow. 2. Quick and easy cookery. I. Hildebrand, Robert. II.
Title. III. Title: Three-ingredient slow cooker comfort foods.
   TX827.H54 2006
   641.5'884--dc22

                                                      2006030390

Original cover design by Ariana Grabec-Dingman
Book design by Yee Design

Printed and bound in Canada

CONTENTS

3-INGREDIENT FREEBIES

As always, we'll give you a few "freebie" ingredients that don't count toward the three-ingredient total in our recipes: water, salt, pepper, oil, and butter. We don't use them in every recipe, but these building-block ingredients serve as a vital foundation that underlies much of our cooking.

Welcome to the wonderful world of slow cooking three-ingredient style! If you're already a slow-cooker aficionado, you'll know that the convenience of slow cooking—having a hot meal ready for you whenever you want it without standing over the stove—is irresistible in today's busy world. In fact, slow cooking recipes have only one drawback—it takes just as long to prep ingredients for a slow-cooked meal as it does a conventional one. After all, you have to spend just as much time gathering and preparing ingredients before putting them into the slow cooker as you would preparing any dish. But no longer. Three-ingredient slow cooking is here to the rescue!

Why Three Ingredients?

With just three ingredients, plus a few basics (see "3-Ingredient Freebies" at left), prep time is reduced to just minutes. (We list the prep time for each recipe in this book, along with the cooking time, so you can see for yourself.) Just grab a few items off the shelf and you're cooking!

Three-ingredient recipes also allow cooks to branch out without freaking out, and you can do so within the comfort zone of a recipe that's not interminably long and complicated. And that's not all. You'll find that grocery shopping will take minutes, not hours, because you can pare the shopping list down to just the essentials.

Three-Ingredient Recipes for the Slow Cooker

To approach writing a book of slow-cooker recipes, we had to learn everything we could about the unique cooking properties of the slow cooker, then adapt our minimalist recipes to take full advantage of the slow cooker's strengths.

Here are some of the things that we learned:

- A slow cooker can be used for much more than soups and stews, but there are limits as to what will work. Broiling? Not so much. Slow-cooker fried chicken is pretty much impossible, too. If you want crispness and browning, or much of any caramelization, you need to add a step to the recipe and do some pre-searing before adding the items to the slow cooker. When our recipes require this step, we let you know and tell you what to do.

- Liquid does not escape from a slow cooker. In fact, it accumulates with enthusiasm, so don't add much unless you are planning on making soup. (We'll give you very precise amounts to add for each recipe.)

- Take your time—or at least leave time to cook. We found that slow cookers are best when used on the low setting. (They aren't called *slow* cookers for nothing!) This generally means that you have to think about dinner before you've had breakfast, or at least by brunch. (We work at home, and have been known to schedule "Prep dinner and put in slow cooker" right into our Outlook calendars.)

■ Slow cookers can be great for making meals when you don't want to heat up the kitchen with the stove. It's mid-July, muggy, and 95°F, you're wilting—time for the slow cooker! It's also a terrific tool for side dishes when stove and oven space is at a premium. They also use much less electricity than your stove does, always pleasing to the frugal-minded.

Once you master the quirks of the slow cooker, it will become a valued and even beloved member of your kitchen equipment fraternity. The idea of returning home to a ready meal and the ease of cleanup have made the slow cooker an enduring favorite.

In the chapters that follow, we'll give you an overview of slow-cooking techniques and staples, then dive into 200 of the most mouthwatering comfort foods you can coax from your slow cooker. From chicken noodle soup to pot roast to mac 'n' cheese to creamy artichoke dip, you'll find your family's favorites in this book—three-ingredient style!

CHAPTER 1

SLOW COOKER BASICS

Short of the microwave, the slow cooker is the ultimate in home-cooking convenience—you just add food, turn it on, and forget about it. When you get home at the end of the day, there's dinner, hot and fragrant and ready to eat.

Well, maybe not *quite* as easy as you think. There's a certain amount of counterintuitive sense involved in using a slow cooker— you actually have to plan ahead to use it, which in turn often involves scheduling cooking time into parts of the day when dicing onions or peeling carrots isn't precisely at the top of your mind. (Brew coffee, pour cereal, cut stew beef—see what we mean?) But there's a huge payoff—the happiness of swinging in the door at the end of the day and smelling the aroma of dinner all ready to serve.

As our lives grow ever busier, the value of having a meal ready on demand is huge. Slow-cooker devotees can get a good meal into their soccer players, evening band-practice attendees, or choir-practice singers without having to resort to the Burger Barn drive-through or a series of brown-bag dinners. And when you're wiped out after a hard day's work, it's a great feeling to know that a healthy home-cooked meal is waiting at the end of your commute.

Slow cookers are specialists, masters of moist, low-heat cooking techniques such as braising and stewing. They will virtually refuse to scorch or burn your food. This can be immensely helpful when plan-ning meals, especially when we add the further dimension of three-ingredient cooking.

In the next eleven chapters, we'll present 200 mouthwatering slow-cooker recipes, ranging from appetizers to desserts. But before we do, let's take a closer look at what slow cookers are, how to use them, and how to stock your pantry with three-ingredient slow cooking in mind.

Slow Cooker Options and Features

The original slow cooker, the Rival Crockpot, was introduced in the 1970s and became a big hit with consumers. The appliance continued to have its place in the American kitchen, but the popularity of slow cookers has soared in recent years, as cooks have discovered that the slow cooker allows them a little relief from the time crucible that so many families battle. Having a home-cooked meal waiting upon returning home provides welcome relief from the hectic pace of today's lifestyle.

Except in appearance, the slow cooker itself has not changed much over the years. In fact, the main concept, whereby food is gently and slowly cooked in a ceramic crock that fits into a surrounding heating element, has not changed one bit. Basic cookers generally have two temperature settings, low and high, and most sport a warm or hold setting as well. The low and high temperature settings are approximately 200°F and 300°F respectively. According to Rival, the low setting is meant for all-day cooking, with 1 hour on high equaling about 2 to 2½ hours of cooking on low. Most have removable crocks that are dishwasher- and oven-safe. Prices range from less than $10 to more than $100.

Our survey of the slow-cooker marketplace reveals a number of available options. The main choices include:

■ **NEW SHAPES AND SIZES.** These appliances come in a wide range of sizes and shapes, from the 1-quart mini pots that are perfect for dips to the 6.5-quart behemoths meant for large roasts or jumbo-size recipes. (You can also frequently find a two-for-one deal, as we've seen a big cooker packaged with a free dip-size cooker.) We tend to like the oval cookers because they accommodate roasts and whole birds, but round cookers in the 3.5- to 5-quart range are generally the most useful all-around choice for a family of four. Slow cookers work best when filled anywhere between halfway and two-thirds full, so use that as a rule of thumb when choosing what size pot you need.

■ **COOL-TOUCH OUTER SURFACE.** Some models stay cool to the touch, even when cooking on high. This is particularly useful for cooks with small children, as it saves inquisitive fingers from a painful burn.

■ **LID LOCKS AND BAGS FOR EASIER TRAVEL.** Many cookers come with an insulated bag that's very useful for keeping food warm during transportation, and lid locks that help secure the food inside the pot. These are both very handy items if you do a lot of potluck dinners and the like.

■ **PROGRAMMABLE TIMERS.** Some of the new higher-end models are fully programmable. Most useful is a feature that automatically switches the cooker to warm after a set cooking time has gone by. The warm setting keeps the food at around 140°F, which is in the safe range for keeping food bacteria-free. Another useful programmable feature lets cooks start the slow cooker on high for an hour, and then automatically switch to the low setting.

■ **NON-CERAMIC AND NONSTICK INSERTS.** Nonstick inserts make cleanup even easier. Non-ceramic models, generally aluminum or steel, are a great bet for cooks who like to get the benefits of caramelization by searing their meat before slow cooking, as they can use the insert itself rather than having to dirty another pan. (Plus, all those good cooked bits that stick to the bottom of the searing pan stay in the cooker and add flavor.)

- **DESIGNER COOKERS.** The decor of slow cookers has moved well beyond the basics — the brown ceramic insert and flowered exterior of the classic '70s slow cooker. Cooks can choose from stainless steel to colors that fit today's kitchen design, or opt for cookers with elegant inserts that can double as lovely serving dishes tableside.

Safe Use of the Slow Cooker

Slow cookers are quite safe if used properly — the heat from the cooker, combined with a generally lengthy cooking time and the steam that builds up under the cooker's tightly fitted top, provides plenty of ammunition to destroy the bacteria that can cause food-borne illnesses. Of course, there are some basic safeguards to take. First, be sure to read through the user manual that comes with your cooker to acquaint yourself with its specific safety recommendations. Once you've read through the manual, follow these basic slow-cooker safety guidelines, unless your manual tells you otherwise:

START CLEAN. Make sure your cooker is clean, as well as your work area. We don't need to tell you to wash your hands before handling food, right? Your mother drummed that into you at an early age. But while cleanliness is good, this does not extend to submerging the exterior of the slow cooker in water — that's a disastrous move with any appliance with a heating element. Instead, sponge off the outer part and wash the insert.

PREPARE INGREDIENTS PROPERLY. Make sure that meat or poultry has been thawed completely before cooking it, as food that is not fully defrosted will impact the cooking time, and cause the meal to spend more time in the food danger zone between 40°F and 140°F, which is prime breeding time for bacteria. Make sure that perishables have been refrigerated until it's time to prepare the meal, to further discourage bacterial proliferation.

Many folks like to do prep work the night before, so they can just throw the meal together quickly in the morning. If you do this, be sure to store meats and veggies separately. *Never* let meat juices touch other foods until it is time to cook. You might also find that some ingredients, such as potatoes or apples, will turn brown when cut up and stored in the fridge overnight.

DON'T PUT COLD FOOD INTO A HOT COOKER. Anybody who has poured a cold drink into a hot glass fresh from the dishwasher knows the danger of combining hot and cold items—it can cause cracking. The same goes with a ceramic insert, so keep cold liquids away from hot cookers. Similarly, don't preheat the slow cooker, or turn it on without food in it—the cold food hitting the hot cooker could cause a crack.

WATCH THE ELECTRICITY. It's not safe to eat food from a slow cooker that's been shut off for any period during the cooking time, so if you come home to blinking clocks, the food will unfortunately have to hit the trash—no matter how thoroughly cooked it looks. It's just too risky, as you'll have no idea how long the food temperature was in the danger zone. (If you're there when the lights go out, that's of course a different story—you can transfer the food to a gas stove or try to find somebody else with power.)

STORE AND REHEAT SAFELY. Don't store leftovers or reheat food in a slow cooker. Leftovers should go into shallow containers that let them cool down more quickly, getting them out of the danger zone as fast as possible. And slow-cooked food can be reheated in a pot on the stove or in the microwave.

Cooking with the Slow Cooker

The slow cooker does differ from other low-heat, moist cooking methods, such as braising, and slow cookery does require some slightly different methods to whip up a truly toothsome dish. Keep these pointers in mind.

First, lighten up on the liquids, unless it's a soup or stew. The slow cooker is a miser with moisture, so you don't need to add as much to begin with as you might with a Dutch oven.

Next, expect vegetables to take longer to cook—the smaller you chop them, the faster they'll cook, so vary the size by the length of time they'll spend in the pot. For instance, if you're going to be gone for 10 hours, the veggies can be cut a little more coarsely then they would if you only had a 6-hour cooking time. Greens are the one exception to this—they can be added in the last hour or so, as they need to heat up only to the ambient temperature to cook.

When you fill your cooker, the veggies go on the bottom and the meat on the top, because the meat cooks faster than the vegetables do. (And in the case of potatoes, they tend to turn gray if they are perched above the meat.)

When it comes to long-cooking recipes that involve grains, opt for long-cooking varieties—brown or converted rice over regular white rice, for example. Those that take more time to cook fit better in a recipe with a lengthy timeline. We do have recipes in this book that use regular long-grain white rice, but the cooking time is less.

Finally, if you want any crispiness or browning on the outside of meats, you'll need to pre-sear the meat before putting it into the slow cooker. It does add an extra step, but it also pays off in deeper flavor and better eye appeal.

Stocking Your Slow-Cooker Pantry

An important part of the three-ingredient credo is finding good-quality prepared foods that bring a lot to the recipe in terms of flavor and variety, and this holds true when cooking with a slow cooker as well. We make use of a number of vegetable blends, sauces, cereals, rice mixes, gravies, and the like.

We have tried hard to find prepared foods that are low in additives and preservatives, a task that has been made easier by the truly startling array of really good prepared foods that burst from grocery shelves these days. In other words, we look for food that is actually *food*. While old standbys such as Velveeta cheese and cream of celery soup certainly have their places, and appear in a few recipes here, they are not the only choices these days.

We try not to specify brands whenever possible, because the truth is that what's out there will vary by region to a certain extent. We use the brands available where we live in New England, but we've tried to make sure that the products used in these recipes are not regional. You should be able to find a reasonable match to anything we are using, whether you're shopping in Tucson or Tuscaloosa. Many times, we found two or three similar products, such as Italian vegetable blend. Our advice is to look at the choices you have and decide which mix you like best.

We found that the following products proved to be staples for building a delicious three-ingredient meal in the slow cooker.

Vegetable Mixes

The frozen food section has come a long way in the past few years, as packagers are expanding the variety of interesting and tasty vegetable combinations, while creating higher quality and taste through better production and freezing methods. Moreover, some of these mixes work even harder by adding sauces—really good sauces, too—right in the package. And some frozen vegetable mixes also contain meat. What this means is that we can create more complex and flavorful recipes while still sticking to three ingredients.

Of course, you can always use fresh veggies in place of frozen—it's a matter of balancing taste and convenience. Usually our preference is for fresh over frozen (and either over canned). But the nature of slow-cooker cuisine dictates that we have a lot of "dump it in and let it go all day" recipes, and frozen and canned ingredients work just fine here. In fact, the slow cooker does a really nice job with frozen vegetables—they stay fairly crisp, and the green ones don't acquire that faded "I lost my chlorophyll" look.

Canned and Bottled Foods

Two foods that have advanced dramatically in terms of quality and variety in recent years are bottled pasta sauces and canned tomatoes. We use both of these products extensively in this book.

Pasta sauces have far outstripped the oversweetened, oversalted versions from early years, and we can now choose from many specialty products with interesting flavor mixes. What used to be called "meat-flavored" (read: little meat at all) sauce has now been joined by sauces with nice chunks of sausage, lots of ground beef, and dozens of mini meatballs. And the advent of bottled Alfredo sauces has opened up all sorts of possibilities for the slow-cooker chef.

Diced, "kitchen-ready" tomatoes are a food category that hardly existed twenty years ago. These are great products, in our opinion, with good flavor and texture. It seems that each time we step into the supermarket, there is a new flavor combo. You can get diced tomatoes with garlic and onion, celery and onion, peppers and onion, lime juice and cilantro, red wine and olive oil, balsamic vinegar and basil … the list goes on. We use lots of these products in this book, and you should feel free to experiment and substitute as your taste dictates.

Prepared Sauces and Marinades

This is another aisle of the supermarket that continually holds new surprises. The quality of Mexican and Asian sauces and meat marinades has improved so much over the years, as has the variety. Experiment and find your favorites! We tend to look at the labels and seek those with the fewest additives, including sugar and sodium.

Meats for the Slow Cooker

Slow cooking is a great way to make use of flavorful but economical cuts of meat. The long, moist, and gentle cooking process is perfect for cuts that are not so tender. Examples include brisket, short ribs, chuck and shoulder of beef, shoulder of pork (smoked or fresh), and lamb shanks. We may call for a particular cut in a recipe, but you can often substitute a similar cut that might be a better deal or more easily found.

We have also found that the slow cooker does a nice job of imitating the slow-roasting oven Bob uses at The Three Stallion Inn for such dishes as prime rib and roast birds. Although you will have to pre-sear the meat to brown it, you will get a nicely cooked piece of meat, evenly done throughout, from the slow cooker.

We know people who view slow cookers through an elitist lens— apparently they consider them to be the bourgeois tools of the masses, something that real cooks don't need to use. To which we respond with a brisk, "Nonsense!" Slow cookers do a job, and they do it well. Not everybody has the time to spend hours preparing complex recipes, and not everybody has the desire or knowledge to do so, either. Many people, however, have the desire to produce healthy and original meals without sacrificing their scant "free" time, and the slow cooker helps them do just that. Once you master the basics of slow cooking, it can help you buy back precious hours of time without sacrificing flavor. And that's good cooking, no matter how you slice it.

CHAPTER 2

APPETIZERS

Slow cookers are a terrific party-planning tool, allowing hosts and hostesses to get some dips and nibbles going ahead of time, and leaving the oven free for more last-minute items. Staggering the prep and cooking of these party foods spreads the workload over a larger time frame, making it far simpler to throw the shindig in the first place. (There's even a 1.5-quart slow cooker available just for dips, an item we recommend—our dip recipes work better with a smaller cooker.) The three-ingredient credo helps streamline the work even more, but the results are always delicious!

● Cheese Fondue

The classic cheeses for this dish are Emmental and Gruyère, but any favorite firm cheese will do. Some like to add a shot of Kirshwasser, a fiery cherry brandy, just before serving.

PREP TIME: 10 minutes

COOKING TIME: 2 hours

ADDITIONAL STEPS: Add the cheese after 1 hour, stir after 1 1/2 hours

INGREDIENTS

- **2 cups (475 ml) white wine**

- **1 pound (455 g) Swiss cheese, cut into small cubes**

- **1/4 cup (30 g) all-purpose flour**

- Salt and pepper to taste

Put the wine in the slow cooker and cook on high for 1 hour. Dredge the cheese in the flour. Add the cheese and flour, plus salt and pepper to taste, to the hot wine. Do not stir. Cover and cook for 1/2 hour. Stir until smooth. Continue to cook for 1/2 hour more. Stir to make sure there are no chunks of unmelted cheese remaining.

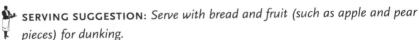 **SERVING SUGGESTION:** *Serve with bread and fruit (such as apple and pear pieces) for dunking.*

YIELD: *4 to 6 servings*

NUTRITIONAL ANALYSIS

357 calories; 21 g fat (61.6% calories from fat); 22g protein; 7g carbohydrate; trace dietary fiber; 69mg cholesterol; 201 mg sodium.

Hot Clam Dip

This will disappear faster than watermelon at a Fourth of July picnic.

PREP TIME: 10 minutes
COOKING TIME: 1¹/₂ hours
ADDITIONAL STEPS: Stir after 1 hour

INGREDIENTS

- **2 (6-ounce or 175-ml) cans minced clams**

- **1 cup (235 ml) bottled Alfredo sauce**

- **1 (8-ounce or 230-g) package cream cheese**

Drain the clams, discarding the juice. Combine the clams, the Alfredo sauce, and the cream cheese in the slow cooker. Cook for 1 hour on high. Stir to combine the ingredients and continue to cook on low for ¹/₂ hour.

 SERVING SUGGESTION: *Serve with chips for dipping.*

YIELD: *10 to 12 as a party dip*

NUTRITIONAL ANALYSIS

148 calories; 11 g fat (65.8% calories from fat); 10g protein; 3g carbohydrate; 0g dietary fiber; 51 mg cholesterol; 198mg sodium.

✚ ADD IT IN!

Stir in a handful of chopped scallions.

🍅 Layered Mexican Dip

Like all the dip recipes, this works best with a 1.5-quart-size slow cooker geared toward dips and such.

PREP TIME: 15 minutes
COOKING TIME: 1¹/₂ hours

INGREDIENTS

- **2 (12-ounce or 390-g) cans refried beans, divided**

- **2 (8-ounce or 200-g) packages whipped cream cheese with chives, divided**

- **1 (16-ounce or 470-ml) jar salsa, divided**

Spread 1 can of the refried beans on the bottom of the slow cooker. Top with half the cream cheese, then half the salsa. Repeat with the remaining 1 can of beans, 1 package cheese, and 8 ounces (235 ml) salsa. Cook on high for 1¹/₂ hours.

 SERVING SUGGESTION: *Serve with tortilla chips for dipping.*

YIELD: *10 to 12 as a party dip*

NUTRITIONAL ANALYSIS

197 calories; 13g fat (59.7% calories from fat); 6g protein; 14g carbohydrate; 4g dietary fiber; 45mg cholesterol; 557mg sodium.

✚ ADD IT IN!

Sprinkle the top with a layer of shredded Monterey Jack cheese for extra tang.

🍅 Spicy Bagna Calda

This classic Italian recipe is great for dunking raw veggies or crusty Italian bread. The gentle heat in a slow cooker keeps the extra-virgin olive oil fragrant and flavorful.

PREP TIME: 10 minutes
COOKING TIME: 2 hours

INGREDIENTS

- **4 anchovy fillets**

- **12 cloves garlic, peeled**

- **1 tablespoon (3.6 g) dried red pepper flakes**

- 3 cups (705 ml) extra-virgin olive oil

Mince the anchovy fillets and, using the side of a chef's knife, mash them into a paste. Lightly smash the garlic cloves with the side of a chef's knife. Combine all the ingredients in the slow cooker and cook on low for 2 hours.

YIELD: *10 to 12 servings as a party dip*

NUTRITIONAL ANALYSIS

485 calories; 54g fat (98.7% calories from fat); 1g protein; 1g carbohydrate; trace dietary fiber; 1mg cholesterol; 50mg sodium.

Spicy Cocktail Franks

If you remember your father in long swoopy sideburns and your mom in poly-ester bell-bottoms, then you are from the Golden Age of the Cocktail Wiener. These yummy little dogs aren't as common at parties these days, but give them a try—they're still one of our favorite guilty pleasures! Don't forget to put out the toothpicks so that guests can serve themselves.

PREP TIME: 10 minutes
COOKING TIME: 3 hours

INGREDIENTS

- **2 medium onions**

- **2 (1-pound or 455-g) packages cocktail franks**

- **1 (12-ounce or 355-ml) jar chili sauce**

Dice the onions into small pieces. Combine the onion, cocktail franks, and chili sauce in the slow cooker and stir. Cook on low for 3 hours.

YIELD: *10 to 12 servings as a party appetizer*

NUTRITIONAL ANALYSIS

255 calories; 22g fat (78.2% calories from fat); 9g protein; 5g carbohydrate; 1g dietary fiber; 38mg cholesterol; 855mg sodium.

Sugar and Spice Walnuts

Sugar and spice and nuts are nice! Cajun spice adds a hot surprise in place of the expected cinnamon. You can substitute pecans or almonds, if you prefer, with equally tasty results.

PREP TIME: 15 minutes
COOKING TIME: 2 hours
ADDITIONAL STEPS: Make the sugar syrup

INGREDIENTS

- **2 cups (400 g) sugar**

- **3 tablespoons (22.5 g) Cajun spice mix**

- **1 pound (455 g) walnut halves**

Turn the slow cooker on high.

Combine the sugar, the spice mix, and 1/2 cup water in a small saucepan. Cook over high heat until the sugar is dissolved. Set aside.

Put the walnuts into a large bowl and pour the sugar syrup over them. Toss to coat the nuts thoroughly. Put them into the slow cooker and cook for 1 to 1 1/2 hours, stirring every half hour, until the nuts are crispy and browned. Cool to room temperature.

YIELD: *8 to 10 servings as a party snack*

NUTRITIONAL ANALYSIS

438 calories; 26g fat (49.8% calories from fat); 11 g protein; 47g carbohydrate; 3g dietary fiber; 0mg cholesterol; 194mg sodium.

Cajun Barbecue Shrimp

These shrimp cooked in spicy melted butter are always a hit. Our cholesterol couldn't take this dish on a daily basis, but it's lip-smacking good. Look for easy-peel shrimp at your grocery store.

PREP TIME: 10 minutes
COOKING TIME: 2 hours
ADDITIONAL STEPS: Add the shrimp in the last hour

INGREDIENTS

- 2 sticks (¹/₂ pound or 225 g) butter

- **¹/₄ cup (30 g) Cajun spice mix**

- **4 tablespoons (40 g) chopped garlic**

- **2 pounds (910 g) shell-on shrimp, thawed if frozen**

Combine the butter, Cajun spice mix, and garlic in the slow cooker. Cook on low for 1 hour. Add the shrimp, stirring to coat with the melted butter and spices. Turn the slow cooker on high. Cook for ¹/₂ to 1 hour, until the shrimp are pink and firm.

 SERVING SUGGESTION: *Serve with bread to mop up the butter (and make sure there are plenty of napkins!).*

YIELD: *8 to 10 as a party appetizer*

NUTRITIONAL ANALYSIS

275 calories; 20g fat (65.8% calories from fat); 19g protein; 4g carbohydrate; 1g dietary fiber; 188mg cholesterol; 580mg sodium.

> **✚ ADD IT IN!**
>
> Toss in a medium tomato, finely chopped.

🍅 Classic Shrimp Cocktail

A slow cooker's gentle heat makes it perfect for poaching shrimp so that they remain plump, moist, and tender. Use good-size shrimp, at 21 to 25 per pound (455 g) or larger, that are shelled and deveined except for the tail.

PREP TIME: 10 minutes
COOKING TIME: 1¹/₂ hours
ADDITIONAL STEPS: Chill the shrimp after poaching

INGREDIENTS

- **2 cups (470 ml) white wine**

- **3 tablespoons (22.5 g) pickling spice mixture**

- Salt and pepper to taste

- **2 pounds (910 g) shrimp, peeled and deveined, with the tail on**

Combine the wine, pickling spice mixture, salt, pepper, and 4 cups (940 ml) of water in the slow cooker. Cook on high for 1 hour. Add the shrimp and reduce to low. Cook for about ¹/₂ hour, until the shrimp are pink, opaque, and firm. Drain the shrimp and chill for at least 2 hours.

 SERVING SUGGESTION: *These are delicious with lemon wedges and cocktail sauce.*

YIELD: *8 to 10 servings as an appetizer*

NUTRITIONAL ANALYSIS

137 calories; 2g fat (18.2% calories from fat); 19g protein; 2g carbohydrate; trace dietary fiber; 138mg cholesterol; 138mg sodium.

🎃 Green Chile Queso Dip

This is much *better than the pre-fab jarred goo. Don't forget to stock up on tortilla chips to go with it!*

PREP TIME: 10 minutes
COOKING TIME: 1¹/₂ hours
ADDITIONAL STEPS: Stir after 1 hour

INGREDIENTS

- **1 pound (455 g) processed cheese, such as Velveeta**

- **2 (4-ounce or 115-g) cans roasted green chiles**

- **1 (5-ounce or 150-ml) can evaporated milk**

Cut the cheese into small cubes and put them into the slow cooker. Drain the chiles and combine with the cheese. Add the evaporated milk. Cook on high for 1 hour. Stir to make smooth and cook for another ¹/₂ hour.

 SERVING SUGGESTION: *Serve with tortilla chips for dipping.*

YIELD: *10 to 12 servings as a party dip*

NUTRITIONAL ANALYSIS

211 calories; 15g fat (60.2% calories from fat); 13g protein; 10g carbohydrate; trace dietary fiber; 51 mg cholesterol; 983mg sodium.

✚ **ADD IT IN!**

Stir in ¹/₂ cup of chopped green scallions to deepen the flavor.

🍅 Hot Spinach Dip

It's funny how many people turn up their noses at spinach—unless it's served in this yummy dip. Our theory is that the cheese somehow cancels out the spinach.

PREP TIME: 10 minutes

COOKING TIME: 2 hours

ADDITIONAL STEPS: Add the cheese in the last hour

INGREDIENTS

- **2 (10-ounce or 280-g) packages frozen chopped spinach**

- **1 (16-ounce or 475-ml) jar Alfredo sauce with garlic**

- **1 cup (80 g) shredded Parmesan cheese**

Combine the frozen spinach and the Alfredo sauce in the slow cooker. (If you're using a small slow cooker, you may need to cut the frozen blocks of spinach in half.) Cook on high for 1 hour. Stir to combine thoroughly. Sprinkle the Parmesan cheese on top and continue to cook, without stirring, for 1 hour.

 SERVING SUGGESTION: *Serve with chips or slices of French bread for dipping.*

YIELD: *6 to 8 servings as a party dip*

NUTRITIONAL ANALYSIS

168 calories; 13g fat (66.8% calories from fat); 9g protein; 6g carbohydrate; 2g dietary fiber; 39mg cholesterol; 524mg sodium.

✚ ADD IT IN!

Stir in a clove or two of chopped garlic to deepen the garlic flavor.

● Blue Cheese Buffalo Wings

Why go to all the bother of dipping your wings into blue cheese dressing? You have better things to do with your time.

PREP TIME: 25 minutes

COOKING TIME: 2 hours

ADDITIONAL STEPS: Pre-broil the wings; add the blue cheese dressing at the end of cooking

INGREDIENTS

- **3 pounds (1365 g) chicken wings**
- **1 cup (235 ml) hot sauce**
- **1 cup (235 ml) blue cheese dressing**

Preheat the broiler. Spread the wings on a baking pan and broil for 10 minutes. Turn and broil another 10 minutes, until crispy.

Combine the wings and the hot sauce in the slow cooker and cook on low for 1½ hours.

Just before serving, stir in the blue cheese dressing.

 SERVING SUGGESTION: *Serve this with a plateful of celery sticks to mop up the extra sauce.*

YIELD: *8 to 10 servings as a party snack*

NUTRITIONAL ANALYSIS

289 calories; 25g fat (76.6% calories from fat); 15g protein; 2g carbohydrate; trace dietary fiber; 71 mg cholesterol; 919mg sodium.

Hot Artichoke Heart Dip

Smooth and creamy, tangy and zesty, this artichoke dip has become a cocktail party classic. Try serving it with pita crisps for dipping.

PREP TIME: 10 minutes
COOKING TIME: 1^1/$_2$ hours
ADDITIONAL STEPS: Process the ingredients to blend

INGREDIENTS

- **2 (14-ounce or 395-g) cans artichoke hearts**

- **2 (8-ounce or 225-g) packages cream cheese**

- **1^1/$_2$ cups (120 g) shredded Parmesan cheese, divided**

- Black pepper to taste

Drain the artichoke hearts and combine them with the cream cheese and half the Parmesan cheese in a food processor. Add black pepper to taste and process until smooth.

Scoop into the slow cooker and top with the remaining ^{3}/$_4$ cup (60 g) cheese. Cook on high for 1^1/$_2$ hours.

YIELD: *12 to 15 servings as a party dip*

NUTRITIONAL ANALYSIS

159 calories; 13g fat (72.3% calories from fat); 7g protein; 4g carbohydrate; 0g dietary fiber; 39mg cholesterol; 357mg sodium.

✚ ADD IT IN!

Stir in a clove or two of chopped garlic to add another dimension.

Teriyaki Wings

Find a nice, thick Teriyaki sauce for this recipe and watch these goodies evaporate into thin air.

PREP TIME: 25 minutes
COOKING TIME: 2 hours 15 minutes
ADDITIONAL STEPS: Broil the wings; add pineapple in the last 15 minutes

INGREDIENTS

- **3 pounds (1365 g) chicken wings**

- **1¹/₂ cups (355 ml) Teriyaki sauce**

- **1 (16-ounce or 455-g) can pineapple chunks (in juice)**

Preheat the broiler. Spread the wings on a baking pan and broil for 10 minutes. Turn and broil another 10 minutes, until crispy.

Combine the wings and the Teriyaki sauce in the slow cooker. Cook on high for 2 hours. Drain the pineapple chunks and stir them gently into the wings. Continue to cook, with the cover off, for 15 minutes.

YIELD: *8 to 10 servings as an appetizer*

NUTRITIONAL ANALYSIS

214 calories; 12g fat (49.7% calories from fat); 16g protein; 11 g carbohydrate; trace dietary fiber; 57mg cholesterol; 1710mg sodium.

CHAPTER 3
SOUPS

Soups and the slow cooker are one of those cookies-and-milk, PB-and-J matches made in heaven. Long, gentle cooking deepens the taste spectrum of many soups, combining different flavors to create a complex and delicious meal. Although we can't help you with the cold summer soups, these delicious hot concoctions will set you up for a cold winter's night, or just help make a busy midweek meal fabulously tasty—no matter what the season.

 Bean and Pasta Soup

We use a mix available in most markets that gives you a wide variety of beans in one soup. You need to start the night before to soak the beans.

PREP TIME: 30 minutes

COOKING TIME: 7–8 hours

ADDITIONAL STEPS: Presoak the beans; par-cook the pasta and add for the last 2 hours of cooking

+ ADD IT IN!

A couple of cloves of chopped garlic, some diced onion, a few chopped carrots, and chopped celery—all would make this soup even yummier.

INGREDIENTS

- **1 pound (455 g) 15-bean soup mix**

- **1 (64-ounce or 1880-ml) can vegetable juice cocktail, such as V-8**

- **4 ounces (115 g) mini-tube pasta (ditalini)**

- Salt and black pepper to taste

Starting at least 12 hours before you plan to make the soup, pick over the beans to remove any debris (such as small stones) and put them into a pan or bowl. Cover with water to twice the depth of the beans. Allow them to soak for at least 12 hours.

Drain the beans and put them into the slow cooker. Add the vegetable juice and 2 cups (475 ml) water. Cook for 6 hours.

Bring a pot of salted water to a boil and add the pasta. Cook the pasta for 6 to 7 minutes, drain, and add to the soup. Continue cooking for 1 to 2 hours, until the beans are soft.

Adjust the seasoning with salt and pepper.

YIELD: *6 to 8 servings*

NUTRITIONAL ANALYSIS

286 calories; 1g fat (3.5% calories from fat); 16g protein; 55g carbohydrate; 16g dietary fiber; 0mg cholesterol; 621 mg sodium.

 # Bean and Vegetable Soup

A good bean soup must be one of the most satisfying meals there is. This vegetable blend we spotted has a nice variety of veggies and beans, such as broccoli, carrots, green beans, white beans, garbanzo beans, and kidney beans. All of this adds up to a bowlful of healthy and tasty soup goodness.

PREP TIME: 30 minutes

COOKING TIME: 6–8 hours

ADDITIONAL STEPS: Cook the bacon

INGREDIENTS

- ½ pound (225 g) bacon, chopped into ½-inch (1-cm) dice

- 1 (16-ounce or 455-g) package Rancho Fiesta Vegetable Blend

- 2 quarts (1890 ml) chicken stock or broth

Cook the bacon in a skillet, the microwave, or the oven. Drain the fat from the bacon and put the bacon into the slow cooker, along with the vegetable blend and the chicken stock. Cook for 6 to 8 hours on low.

YIELD: *6 to 8 servings*

NUTRITIONAL ANALYSIS

206 calories; 14g fat (67.7% calories from fat); 10g protein; 5g carbohydrate; 2g dietary fiber; 24mg cholesterol; 2727mg sodium.

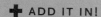 **ADD IT IN!**

Sprinkle a little finely grated Parmesan cheese on top of each bowl of soup before serving.

🍲 Beef Barley Soup

The starch from the barley makes for a full, rich, satisfying broth.

PREP TIME: 30 minutes
COOKING TIME: 8 hours
ADDITIONAL STEPS: Add the vegetables for the last 2 hours of cooking

INGREDIENTS

- **2 pounds (910 g) stew beef**

- Salt and pepper to taste

- **2 cups (400 g) pearl barley**

- **1 (16-ounce or 455-g) package frozen broccoli, cauliflower, and carrot mix**

Cut the stew beef into smaller pieces and put them into the slow cooker. Season with salt and pepper. Add the barley and 8 cups (1880 ml) water. Cook for 6 hours on low. Stir, using the spoon to shred the beef. Add the vegetables and cook for 2 hours more. Adjust the seasoning with salt and pepper.

YIELD: *6 to 8 servings*

NUTRITIONAL ANALYSIS

536 calories; 24g fat (40.5% calories from fat); 38g protein; 42g carbohydrate; 10g dietary fiber; 113mg cholesterol; 351 mg sodium.

✚ ADD IT IN!

A couple of bay leaves or other fresh herbs, such as chopped fresh oregano, would flavor the broth nicely.

Cabbage Soup with Kielbasa

Rich in vitamin C, cabbage is both good and good for you, as this recipe attests.
Try to find a low-fat sausage for even healthier eating.

PREP TIME: 30 minutes
COOKING TIME: 6–8 hours

INGREDIENTS

- **1 pound (455 g) kielbasa sausage**

- **1/2 head green cabbage**

- **1 (64-ounce or 1880-ml) can vegetable juice cocktail, such as V-8**

Cut the kielbasa into 1/2-inch-thick rings and put them into the slow cooker. Finely shred the cabbage; you should have about 4 cups (280 g). Add the cabbage to the cooker. Pour the vegetable juice over all. Cook for 6 to 8 hours on low.

YIELD: *6 to 8 servings*

NUTRITIONAL ANALYSIS

220 calories; 16g fat (62.8% calories from fat); 9g protein; 12g carbohydrate; 2g dietary fiber; 38mg cholesterol; 1224mg sodium.

Chicken, Broccoli, and Ale Soup

This easy soup is sure to please, and it makes a delicious dinner with some warm rolls and a green salad.

PREP TIME: 15 minutes
COOKING TIME: 6–8 hours

INGREDIENTS

- **1 pound (455 g) boneless, skinless chicken breasts**

- **1 (16-ounce or 455-g) package frozen broccoli in cheese sauce**

- **1 (12-ounce or 355-ml) bottle beer**

- Salt and pepper to taste

Cut the chicken into small pieces and put into the slow cooker. Add the broccoli and the beer, along with 4 cups (940 ml) water. Cook for 6 to 8 hours on low. Stir well, breaking up some of the broccoli into the soup. Season with salt and pepper to taste.

YIELD: *4 to 6 servings*

NUTRITIONAL ANALYSIS

132 calories; 2g fat (16.5% calories from fat); 19g protein; 6g carbohydrate; 2g dietary fiber; 46mg cholesterol; 61 mg sodium.

✚ ADD IT IN!

Stir in 1 cup (115 g) of shredded cheddar cheese for even more cheesy tang.

 # Chicken Noodle Soup

This one has some additional steps, but the results are all you could want in a chicken soup. It's guaranteed to cure common colds, evening grumps, and general sick-of-winter blues.

PREP TIME: 45 minutes

COOKING TIME: 10 hours

ADDITIONAL STEPS: Remove the chicken meat from the bones after cooking; par-cook the noodles; add the noodles and vegetables during the last 2 hours of cooking

INGREDIENTS

- **1 chicken (about 3 pounds or 1365 g)**

- **¹/₂ pound (225 g) egg noodles**

- **1 (16-ounce or 455-g) bag frozen mixed vegetables**

- Salt and pepper to taste

Cut the chicken into 4 pieces, removing the skin. Put the chicken, along with the neck, into the slow cooker. Season with salt and pepper. Add 10 cups (2350 ml) water and cook on low for 8 hours.

Remove the chicken from the cooker and allow to cool. Leave the broth in the cooker. Bring a pot of salted water to a boil and cook the noodles for 6 minutes. Drain the noodles and add them to the cooker. Add the vegetables. When the chicken is cool enough to handle, remove the meat from the bones, discarding the bones. Discard the neck. Shred the chicken meat and return it to the cooker. Cook for another 2 hours on low. Adjust the seasoning and serve.

YIELD: *8 to 10 servings*

NUTRITIONAL ANALYSIS

248 calories; 16g fat (57.3% calories from fat); 19g protein; 8g carbohydrate; 2g dietary fiber; 91 mg cholesterol; 90mg sodium.

 Chicken Soup with Pasta

This cozy concoction is delicious and popular with grown-ups and small-fry alike.

PREP TIME: 20 minutes
COOKING TIME: 6–8 hours

INGREDIENTS

- 1 pound (455 g) boneless, skinless chicken breasts

- 1 (16-ounce or 455-g) bag frozen vegetable and pasta blend

- 2 quarts (1890 ml) chicken stock or broth

- Salt and pepper to taste

Cut the chicken into small cubes and put the pieces into the slow cooker. Add the vegetable and pasta blend and the stock. Season with salt and pepper, and cook for 6 to 8 hours on low. Adjust the seasoning and serve.

YIELD: *6 to 7 servings*

NUTRITIONAL ANALYSIS

168 calories; 2g fat (13.6% calories from fat); 18g protein; 15g carbohydrate; 2g dietary fiber; 40mg cholesterol; 2504mg sodium.

Creamy Black Bean and Tomato Soup

This tangy soup has a Tex-Mex flair that takes it from merely good to simply terrific.

PREP TIME: 15 minutes
COOKING TIME: 6–8 hours

INGREDIENTS

- **2 (14-ounce or 395-g) cans diced tomatoes with lime juice, cilantro, and jalapeños**

- **1 (16-ounce or 455-g) can black beans**

- **1 (8-ounce or 235-ml) can evaporated milk**

- Salt and pepper to taste

Put all the ingredients plus 2 cups (470 ml) water into the slow cooker. Stir. Cook for 6 to 8 hours on low. Adjust the seasoning with salt and pepper to taste.

YIELD: *6 to 8 servings*

NUTRITIONAL ANALYSIS

101 calories; 3g fat (23.5% calories from fat); 6g protein; 14g carbohydrate; 3g dietary fiber; 8mg cholesterol; 602mg sodium.

 ADD IT IN!

Sprinkle chopped fresh cilantro over the bowls of soup just before serving.

Easy Manhattan Clam Chowder

As good New Englanders, we must uphold the Yankee Oath of Fealty we took at birth regarding clam chowder: Milk-based chowder is, and always will be, superior. That said, we like the red kind, too. Here is an easy way to have some.

PREP TIME: 20 minutes
COOKING TIME: 6–8 hours

INGREDIENTS

- **2 pounds (910 g) boiling potatoes, such as Yukon Gold**
- **2 (12-ounce or 355-ml) bottles clam juice**
- **2 (14-ounce or 425-ml) cans red clam sauce**
- Salt and pepper to taste

Peel the potatoes and cut them into small cubes. Put the potatoes into the slow cooker. Add the clam juice, the red clam sauce, and 3 cups (705 ml) water. Cook for 6 to 8 hours on low, until the potatoes are nice and soft. Season with salt and pepper to taste.

YIELD: *4 to 6 servings*

NUTRITIONAL ANALYSIS

309 calories; 10g fat (27.5% calories from fat); 10g protein; 48g carbohydrate; 3g dietary fiber; 16mg cholesterol; 1129mg sodium.

✚ ADD IT IN!

Stir 1/2 cup (50 g) chopped celery into the mix.

Hot and Sour Chinese Vegetable Soup

This is not the same recipe as the hot and sour soup found in your favorite restaurant, but it's quite tasty in its own right.

PREP TIME: 15 minutes
COOKING TIME: 8 hours
ADDITIONAL STEPS: Add the vegetables for the final hour of cooking

INGREDIENTS

- **1 (64-ounce or 1880-ml) can beef broth**

- **1 (10-ounce or 285-ml) jar Szechuan stir-fry sauce**

- **1 (16-ounce or 455-g) package frozen Szechuan or stir-fry vegetables**

- Salt and pepper to taste

Combine the beef broth and the stir-fry sauce in the slow cooker. Cook for 7 hours on low. Add the vegetables and cook for an additional hour. Adjust the seasoning with salt and pepper.

YIELD: *6 to 8 servings*

NUTRITIONAL ANALYSIS

106 calories; 0g fat (0.0% calories from fat); 13g protein; 14g carbohydrate; 1g dietary fiber; 0mg cholesterol; 2294mg sodium.

Italian Meatball and Pasta Soup

PREP TIME: 30 minutes
COOKING TIME: 4–6 hours
ADDITIONAL STEPS: Par-cook the pasta

INGREDIENTS

- 4 ounces (115 g) penne pasta

- 1 (16-ounce or 455-g) jar pasta sauce with mini-meatballs

- 1 quart (945 ml) beef broth

- Salt and pepper to taste

Bring a pot of salted water to a boil. Add the penne and cook for 6 minutes. Drain the pasta and put it into the slow cooker. Add the pasta sauce and the beef broth. Cook on low for 4 to 6 hours. Adjust the seasoning with salt and pepper.

YIELD: *4 to 6 servings*

NUTRITIONAL ANALYSIS

165 calories; 5g fat (27.3% calories from fat); 12g protein; 18g carbohydrate; 1g dietary fiber; 7mg cholesterol; 984mg sodium.

✚ ADD IT IN!

Chop up a handful of fresh basil leaves and stir them in with the pasta sauce.

Lentil and Tomato Soup

Lentils are one of those foods that don't jump right out at most meal planners, but they also seem to garner rave reviews when they do make an appearance at the dinner table. Not only are they packed with iron and protein, but they are also far cheaper than many other protein sources. (T-bone steak, we're looking at you.)

PREP TIME: 10 minutes
COOKING TIME: 6–8 hours

INGREDIENTS

- **1¹⁄₂ quarts (1425 ml) chicken stock or broth**

- **2 cups (400 g) dried lentils**

- **1 (14-ounce or 395-g) can diced tomatoes with onion and celery**

- Salt and pepper to taste

Wash the lentils in a colander and pick them over for any small pebbles. Add all of the ingredients to the slow cooker. Cook for 6 to 8 hours on low, until the lentils are soft. Adjust the seasoning with salt and pepper to taste.

YIELD: *6 to 8 servings*

NUTRITIONAL ANALYSIS

188 calories; 1g fat (3.2% calories from fat); 15g protein; 30g carbohydrate; 15g dietary fiber; 0mg cholesterol; 1689mg sodium.

> ✚ ADD IT IN!
>
> Add in 1 cup (130 g) chopped carrots.

 Pumpkin Soup

This harvest favorite is a wonderful treat when the leaves start to turn. You can substitute any winter squash for the pumpkin with equally delightful results.

PREP TIME: 15 minutes
COOKING TIME: 6–8 hours
ADDITIONAL STEPS: Puree soup after cooking

INGREDIENTS

- **2 medium onions**

- **2 (14-ounce or 395-g) cans pumpkin puree**

- **1 quart (945 ml) apple cider**

- Salt and pepper to taste

Peel the onions and dice them into small pieces. Put the chopped onion into the slow cooker. Add the pumpkin and the cider. Cook for 6 to 8 hours on low. Puree using an immersion blender, or puree in batches in a blender or food processor. Season with salt and pepper to taste. Add water to thin the soup, if necessary

YIELD: *6 to 8 servings*

NUTRITIONAL ANALYSIS

102 calories; trace fat (3.7% calories from fat); 1g protein; 25g carbohydrate; 3g dietary fiber; 0mg cholesterol; 10mg sodium.

✚ ADD IT IN!

Add ½ teaspoon (1.1 g) nutmeg to the soup.

 # Quick Shrimp Bisque

Bisques make an elegant starter for a dinner party, and this one is ready to go when you are—no last-minute work necessary. Bon appétit!

PREP TIME: 15 minutes

COOKING TIME: 4 hours

ADDITIONAL STEPS: Blend the soup after cooking

INGREDIENTS

- **2 (10-ounce or 285-ml) bottles clam juice**

- **2 (10-ounce or 280-g) bottles shrimp in cocktail sauce**

- **2 (8-ounce or 235-ml) cans evaporated milk**

- Salt and pepper to taste

Put the clam juice, the shrimp and cocktail sauce, and the evaporated milk into the slow cooker. Cook for 4 hours on low. Blend with an immersion blender or in batches in a blender or food processor. Adjust the seasoning with salt and pepper.

YIELD: *4 to 6 servings*

NUTRITIONAL ANALYSIS

245 calories; 7g fat (27.7% calories from fat); 25g protein; 19g carbohydrate; trace dietary fiber; 166mg cholesterol; 598mg sodium.

Sausage and Vegetable Soup

Rich tomato broth simmered with Italian sausage and vegetables makes for a delicious and hearty meal.

PREP TIME: 30 minutes
COOKING TIME: 6–8 hours

INGREDIENTS

- **1 pound (455 g) sweet Italian sausage links**
- **1 (16-ounce or 455-g) package Italian vegetable blend**
- **1 (64-ounce or 1880-ml) can tomato juice**
- Salt and pepper to taste

Slice the sausages into ½-inch (1-cm) rounds and put them into the slow cooker. Add the vegetables and the tomato juice. Cook on low for 6 to 8 hours on low. Adjust the seasoning with salt and pepper.

YIELD: *6 to 8 servings*

NUTRITIONAL ANALYSIS

271 calories; 18g fat (58.3% calories from fat); 12g protein; 18g carbohydrate; 5g dietary fiber; 43mg cholesterol; 1260mg sodium.

 ADD IT IN!

Use vegetable juice cocktail, such as V-8, instead of tomato juice.

 Onion Soup

Fragrant, piping-hot onion soup—what a wonderful way to greet a chilly night! This soup is delicious as a first course, or it can be a light meal with a salad and crusty bread.

PREP TIME: 30 minutes
COOKING TIME: 8 hours
ADDITIONAL STEPS: Add wine and broth after 4 hours

INGREDIENTS

- **2 pounds (910 g) yellow or Spanish onions**

- 3 tablespoons (45 g) butter

- **1 cup (235 ml) red wine**

- **1 (64-ounce or 1880-ml) can beef broth**

- Salt and pepper to taste

Peel the onions and slice them very thin. Put the onions and the butter into the slow cooker. Cook on low for 4 hours, until the onions are very soft and a little caramelized. Add the red wine and the beef broth. Cook for another 4 hours on low. Adjust the seasoning with salt and pepper to taste.

YIELD: *6 to 8 servings*

NUTRITIONAL ANALYSIS

157 calories; 4g fat (28.9% calories from fat); 11 g protein; 14g carbohydrate; 2g dietary fiber; 12mg cholesterol; 1246mg sodium.

✚ ADD IT IN!

Some cheese melted on top of the soup gives it that French onion soup feel.

 Zesty Clam Chowder

This recipe is a little spicier than most clam chowders, thanks to the addition of garlic in the white clam sauce.

PREP TIME: 20 minutes
COOKING TIME: 6–8 hours

INGREDIENTS

- **2 pounds (910 g) boiling potatoes**

- **1 (16-ounce or 470-ml) jar Alfredo sauce**

- **2 (10-ounce or 285-ml) cans white clam sauce**

Peel the potatoes and cut them into small cubes. Put the potatoes and 1 cup (235 ml) water into the slow cooker. Add the Alfredo sauce and the clam sauce. Stir. Cook for 6 to 8 hours on low.

YIELD: *4 to 6 servings*

NUTRITIONAL ANALYSIS

357 calories; 19g fat (46.4% calories from fat); 13g protein; 36g carbohydrate; 2g dietary fiber; 58mg cholesterol; 767mg sodium

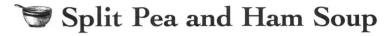 Split Pea and Ham Soup

This country classic is always a hit at the dinner table, even with folks who generally eschew anything green.

PREP TIME: 20 minutes

COOKING TIME: 6–8 hours

INGREDIENTS

- **½ pound (225 g) cooked ham**

- **1 medium onion**

- **1 pound (455 g) split green peas**

- Salt and pepper to taste

Cut the ham into ¼-inch (6-mm) cubes and put them into the slow cooker. Peel the onion and dice it into small pieces. Add the onion to the ham. Rinse the peas and pick through them to remove any small stones or other debris. Add the peas and 8 cups (1880 ml) water to the slow cooker. Cook for 6 to 8 hours on low. The peas should be very soft. Stir the soup to break up some of the peas and thicken the soup. Adjust the seasoning with salt and pepper.

YIELD: *6 to 8 servings*

NUTRITIONAL ANALYSIS

250 calories; 4g fat (13.0% calories from fat); 19g protein; 36g carbohydrate; 15g dietary fiber; 16mg cholesterol; 383mg sodium.

 # Tomato Salmon Bisque

This is a rich and delicious soup that is so easy to make. Try to find a really good-quality tomato soup to use as a base for the recipe—we recommend those soups that come in cardboard cartons, generally found in the natural foods section of the grocery store.

PREP TIME: 10 minutes

COOKING TIME: 3–4 hours

ADDITIONAL STEPS: Blend the soup and stir in the cheese at the end of cooking

INGREDIENTS

- **1 quart (945 ml) tomato soup (not condensed)**

- **1 (12-ounce or 340-g) can salmon**

- **2 cups (225 g) shredded cheddar cheese**

- Salt and pepper to taste

Put the tomato soup and the salmon into the slow cooker. Cook for 3 to 4 hours on low. Blend the soup with an immersion blender or blend in batches in a blender or food processor. Stir in the cheese until it has melted and the soup is smooth. Adjust the seasoning with salt and pepper.

YIELD: *4 to 6 servings*

NUTRITIONAL ANALYSIS

287 calories; 17g fat (53.6% calories from fat); 22g protein; 12g carbohydrate; trace dietary fiber; 71 mg cholesterol; 1011mg sodium.

 ADD IT IN!

Sprinkle a bit of chopped dill over each bowl before serving.

Vegetarian White Bean and Escarole Soup

Escarole is one of those dark green leafy vegetables so beloved by nutritional experts and so neglected by many cooks. This take on a classic Italian soup will help you bring this delicious vegetable into your mainstream menu.

PREP TIME: 20 minutes
COOKING TIME: 6–8 hours

INGREDIENTS

- **1 small head escarole**

- **2 quarts (1890 ml) vegetable stock or broth**

- **1 (20-ounce or 560-g) can large white beans**

- Salt and pepper to taste

Chop the escarole into small pieces and wash it well. Drain and add the escarole to the slow cooker. Add the vegetable stock. Pour the beans into a colander. Rinse, drain, and add them to the cooker. Season with salt and pepper to taste. Cook on low for 6 to 8 hours.

YIELD: *6 to 8 servings*

NUTRITIONAL ANALYSIS

257 calories; 4g fat (14.2% calories from fat); 12g protein; 44g carbohydrate; 8g dietary fiber; 2mg cholesterol; 1642mg sodium.

+ ADD IT IN!

If you're not a vegetarian, you can use chicken stock or broth if you prefer. Try stirring in some fresh chopped thyme for a deeper burst of flavor.

 Beef Borscht

In this recipe, we take a prepared product and transform it into a hearty meal. Serve with crusty pumpernickel bread and a crisp salad for a warming winter repast.

PREP TIME: 10 minutes
COOKING TIME: 7–8 hours
ADDITIONAL STEPS: Break up the meat after cooking

INGREDIENTS

- **1 pound (455 g) beef stew meat**

- **1 quart (945 ml) prepared borscht**

- **1 cup (230 g) sour cream**

Put the beef into the slow cooker and add the borscht. Cook on low for 7 to 8 hours. Break up the meat into shreds using tongs or a slotted spoon. Serve with a dollop of sour cream on top.

YIELD: *4 servings*

NUTRITIONAL ANALYSIS

388 calories; 22g fat (51.2% calories from fat); 28g protein; 19g carbohydrate; 3g dietary fiber; 88mg cholesterol; 226mg

CHAPTER 4
CHICKEN

Chicken was once the costly special-occasion meat, reserved for holidays or Sunday dinners. Things have changed; the wholesale price of a roaster fell by 50 percent from 1978 to 2000. And as the price dropped, chicken's popularity skyrocketed. Chicken's versatility, along with its ease of preparation, makes it a perfect dish for today's time-crunched cooks. Slow cooking chicken can help ease a cook's time pressure while still preserving the taste and convenience of many chicken dishes. In this chapter, we range from stews to whole roasted birds, all rich in flavor and simple to make. There's nothing better than coming home to the mouthwatering aroma of Lemon Rosemary "Roast" Chicken (page 74), except knowing that most of the work has already been done!

Cheesy Chicken, Potato, and Broccoli Bake

This homey casserole-type dinner is an all-in-one meal that's great with a simple salad.

PREP TIME: 30 minutes

COOKING TIME: 2–3 hours on high or 5–6 hours on low

ADDITIONAL STEPS: Stir after 2 hours

INGREDIENTS

- **2 pounds (910 g) boneless, skinless chicken breasts**

- **3 pounds (1365 g) small red potatoes**

- **1 (16-ounce or 455-g) package broccoli with cheese sauce**

Cut the chicken into 1- to 2-inch (2.5- to 5-cm) pieces. Put them into the slow cooker. Cut the potatoes in half and add to the chicken. Add the broccoli and cheese sauce. Cook for 2 to 3 hours on high or 5 to 6 hours on low, stirring after 2 hours.

YIELD: *4 to 6 servings*

NUTRITIONAL ANALYSIS

384 calories; 5g fat (12.1% calories from fat); 40g protein; 44g carbohydrate; 5g dietary fiber; 95mg cholesterol; 186mg sodium.

✚ ADD IT IN!

Stir in some shredded fresh cheddar for an even cheesier tang.

Chicken and Artichoke Casserole

With artichokes firmly ensconced in the Hildebrand Pantheon of all-time favorite vegetables, small wonder that we love this—it's creamy, delicious, and easy to make. Serve with rice pilaf or over pasta.

PREP TIME: 15 minutes

COOKING TIME: 2 hours on high or 4–5 hours on low

INGREDIENTS

- **2 pounds (910 g) boneless, skinless chicken breasts**

- **1 (14-ounce or 395-g) can artichoke hearts, drained**

- **1 (12-ounce or 355-ml) can condensed cream of mushroom soup**

Cut the chicken breasts into 2-inch (5-cm) pieces and put them into the slow cooker. Cut the artichoke hearts in half and add them to the chicken. Add the cream of mushroom soup. Cook for 2 hours on high or 4 to 5 hours on low. Stir and serve.

YIELD: *4 servings*

NUTRITIONAL ANALYSIS

363 calories; 9g fat (23.0% calories from fat); 55g protein; 14g carbohydrate; 6g dietary fiber; 139mg cholesterol; 574mg sodium.

✚ ADD IT IN!

Quarter a handful of white (button) mushrooms and stir them into the mix.

Chicken and Dumplings

This home-style favorite adapts beautifully to the slow cooker.

PREP TIME: 40 minutes
COOKING TIME: 3 hours on high or 5–6 hours on low
ADDITIONAL STEPS: Brown the chicken; mix and add the dumplings in the last hour of cooking

INGREDIENTS

- **1 fryer chicken, cut up into 8 pieces, or 8 to10 chicken pieces (about 4 pounds or 1820 g)**

- Salt and pepper to taste

- Cooking oil

- **2 teaspoons (5 g) poultry seasoning mix**

- **2 cups (250 g) self-rising flour**

- ¹/₂ cup (100 g) shortening, such as Crisco

Season the chicken pieces with salt and pepper. Heat a large sauté pan over medium-high heat and add a couple of tablespoons (30 ml) of oil. Sear the chicken on all sides to brown well, cooking in batches, if needed, to avoid crowding the pieces. Put the seared chicken into the slow cooker. Add the poultry seasoning and 3 cups (705 ml) water. Cook for 2 hours on high or 4 to 5 hours on low.

Put the self-rising flour and the shortening into a mixing bowl. Cut the shortening into the flour. Stir in enough water to form a dough, and drop the dough by spoonfuls into the slow cooker. Cook for another hour. Serve pieces of chicken with some of the broth and a few dumplings in bowls.

YIELD: *4 to 6 servings*

NUTRITIONAL ANALYSIS

835 calories; 56g fat (61.8% calories from fat); 47g protein; 31 g carbohydrate; 1g dietary fiber; 226mg cholesterol; 703mg sodium.

✚ ADD IT IN!

Toss a couple of handfuls of baby carrots into the pot for a one-stop meal.

Chicken and Potatoes in Tomato Sauce

Here is a delicious and hearty meal to greet you on your return home.

PREP TIME: 30 minutes
COOKING TIME: 3 hours on high or 5–6 hours on low
ADDITIONAL STEPS: Brown the chicken pieces before adding to the slow cooker

INGREDIENTS

- **1 fryer chicken, cut up into 8 pieces, or 8 to10 chicken pieces (about 4 pounds or 1820 g)**

- Salt and pepper to taste

- Cooking oil

- **3 pounds (1365 g) potatoes**

- **1 (14-ounce or 395-g) can diced tomatoes with celery and onion**

Season the chicken pieces with salt and pepper. Heat a large sauté pan over medium-high heat and add a couple of tablespoons (30 ml) of oil. Sear the chicken on all sides to brown well, cooking in batches, if needed, to avoid crowding the pieces.

Peel the potatoes and slice them about $\frac{1}{2}$ inch (1 cm) thick. Add the potatoes to the cooker. Put the seared chicken into the slow cooker. Add the diced tomatoes. Cook for 3 hours on high or 5 to 6 hours on low. Serve pieces of chicken with some of the potatoes and sauce.

YIELD: *4 to 6 servings*

NUTRITIONAL ANALYSIS

729 calories; 39g fat (48.9% calories from fat); 48g protein; 44g carbohydrate; 4g dietary fiber; 226mg cholesterol; 193mg sodium.

✚ ADD IT IN!

Sprinkle in a handful of chopped fresh oregano.

Chicken and Spinach Tikka Masala

This dish is a rich, flavorful Indian favorite. Serve with basmati rice and some fresh cilantro sprinkled over each serving.

PREP TIME: 20 minutes

COOKING TIME: 3 hours on high or 5–6 hours on low

ADDITIONAL STEPS: Thaw and squeeze out the spinach before adding to the cooker

INGREDIENTS

- **2 (10-ounce or 280-g) packages frozen spinach**

- **3 pounds (1365 g) boneless, skinless chicken breasts**

- **1 (16-ounce or 475-ml) jar tikka masala cooking sauce**

Thaw the spinach and squeeze out as much water as possible. Put the spinach into the slow cooker. Cut the chicken into 1- to 2-inch (2.5- to 5-cm) pieces and add to the slow cooker. Pour the tikka masala sauce over all. Cook for 3 hours on high or 5 to 6 hours on low. Stir to combine all the ingredients well.

YIELD: *6 to 8 servings*

NUTRITIONAL ANALYSIS

526 calories; 34g fat (58.5% calories from fat); 44g protein; 10g carbohydrate; 6g dietary fiber; 113mg cholesterol; 1776mg sodium.

Chicken Vegetable Stuffing-Topped Casserole

In the great debate over whether outside stuffing is better than inside stuffing, we'd like to add this slow-cooker candidate for consideration.

PREP TIME: 45 minutes

COOKING TIME: 2–3 hours on high or 5–6 hours on low

ADDITIONAL STEPS: Sear the chicken pieces before adding to the slow cooker; mix the stuffing before adding to the slow cooker

INGREDIENTS

- **1 fryer chicken, cut up into 8 pieces, or 8 to 10 chicken pieces (about 4 pounds or 1820 g)**

- Salt and pepper to taste

- Cooking oil

- **1 (1-pound or 455-g) bag Italian broccoli vegetable mix**

- **1 (12-ounce or 340-g) package stuffing mix**

- 4 tablespoons (¹/₂ stick or 55 g) butter or margarine

 ➕ ADD IT IN!

Stir some Bell's Poultry Seasoning into the stuffing mix along with the butter and water.

Season the chicken pieces with salt and pepper. Heat a large sauté pan over medium-high heat and add a couple of tablespoons (30 ml) of oil. Sear the chicken on all sides to brown well, cooking in batches, if needed, to avoid crowding the pieces.

Put the seared chicken into the slow cooker and add the vegetables. Put the stuffing mix into a large bowl. Melt the butter over low heat and stir in 1 cup (235 ml) warm water. Stir the liquid into the stuffing mix. Spoon the stuffing on top of the chicken and vegetables in the slow cooker. Cook for 2 to 3 hours on high or 5 to 6 hours on low.

Serve some of the stuffing along with the chicken and vegetables.

YIELD: *4 to 6 servings*

NUTRITIONAL ANALYSIS

871 calories; 49g fat (51.0% calories from fat); 52g protein; 54g carbohydrate; 5g dietary fiber; 248mg cholesterol; 1189mg sodium.

Chicken Breasts with Endive

Belgian endive is chiefly seen as a handy dip or mousse container, but that wastes its true talent. This is a vegetable that, in our humble opinion, is better cooked than raw, because it develops a much deeper and sweeter flavor. The slow cooker is a perfect vehicle to produce soft and buttery endive.

PREP TIME: 30 minutes

COOKING TIME: 3 hours on high or 5–6 hours on low

ADDITIONAL STEPS: Sear the chicken breasts before adding to the slow cooker

INGREDIENTS

- **4 pieces chicken breasts, bone-in and skin on (about 2$\frac{1}{2}$ pounds or 1140 g)**

- Salt and pepper to taste

- Cooking oil

- **4 heads Belgian endive**

- **1 cup (235 ml) chicken stock or broth**

Season the chicken breasts with salt and pepper. Heat a large sauté pan over medium-high heat and add a couple of tablespoons (30 ml) of oil. Sear the chicken, skin side down, until well browned. Turn and brown the other side. While the chicken is cooking, split the endive lengthwise in half and add to the slow cooker. Put the chicken on top and pour the stock over all. Cook for 3 hours on high or 5 to 6 hours on low.

Serve the chicken with some of the endive and pan juices.

YIELD: *4 servings*

NUTRITIONAL ANALYSIS

428 calories; 8g fat (17.9% calories from fat); 70g protein; 17g carbohydrate; 16g dietary fiber; 173mg cholesterol; 800mg sodium.

 # Chicken Breasts with Sour Cherries

The sour cream added at the end of this recipe makes for a smooth and flavorful sauce.

PREP TIME: 30 minutes

COOKING TIME: 3 hours on high or 5–6 hours on low

ADDITIONAL STEPS: Sear the chicken pieces before adding to the slow cooker; degrease the sauce; stir in sour cream just before serving

INGREDIENTS

- **4 pieces chicken breasts, bone-in and skin on (about 2¹/₂ pounds or 1140 g)**

- Salt and pepper to taste

- Cooking oil

- **1 cup (155 g) bottled drained sour cherries, with ¹/₂ cup (120 ml) of the juice reserved**

- **1 cup (230 g) sour cream**

Season the chicken breasts with salt and pepper. Heat a large sauté pan over medium-high heat and add about 2 tablespoons (30 ml) of oil. Sear the chicken, skin side down, until well browned. Turn and brown the other side. Put the chicken breasts into the slow cooker and add the cherries and the reserved juice. Cook for 3 hours on high or 5 to 6 hours on low. Remove the chicken and keep it warm. Degrease the sauce with a ladle. Stir the sour cream into the sauce. Serve the chicken breasts with some of the sauce and cherries poured over the top.

YIELD: *4 servings*

NUTRITIONAL ANALYSIS

480 calories; 19g fat (37.4% calories from fat); 65g protein; 8g carbohydrate; 1g dietary fiber; 199mg cholesterol; 185mg sodium.

Chicken Cacciatore

You can add your own dimension to this dish with the sauce that you choose—there are several that feature peppers, if you really want to emphasize the pepper taste here.

PREP TIME: 45 minutes
COOKING TIME: 2–3 hours on high or 5–6 hours on low
ADDITIONAL STEPS: Sear the chicken pieces before adding to the slow cooker; sauté the peppers before adding to the slow cooker

✚ ADD IT IN!

Toss 2 cups (140 g) quartered white (button) mushrooms into the pot along with the rest of the ingredients. Pitted black kalamata olives would also work nicely.

INGREDIENTS

- **1 fryer chicken, cut up into 8 pieces, or 8 to10 chicken pieces (about 2¹/₂ pounds or 1140 g)**

- Salt and pepper to taste

- Cooking oil

- **1 (10-ounce or 280-g) bag frozen pepper stir-fry mix**

- **2 cups (490 g) marinara sauce**

Season the chicken pieces with salt and pepper. Heat a large sauté pan over medium-high heat and add a couple of tablespoons (30 ml) of oil. Sear the chicken on all sides to brown well, cooking in batches, if needed, to avoid crowding the pieces.

Put the seared chicken into the slow cooker. Sauté the pepper mix in the same sauté pan for 4 to 5 minutes, and then add to the slow cooker. Pour the marinara sauce over all. Cook for 2 to 3 hours on high or 5 to 6 hours on low. Serve in shallow bowls so you can serve some of the pan juices with the chicken and vegetables.

YIELD: *4 to 6 servings*

NUTRITIONAL ANALYSIS

600 calories; 41 g fat (62.1% calories from fat); 45g protein; 10g carbohydrate; 2g dietary fiber; 226mg cholesterol; 525mg sodium.

 # Chicken in Salsa Verde

Salsa verde, or green salsa, is made from tomatillos. The tomatillo is a bright green cousin to the tomato and is typically covered in a paperlike husk. These tangy veggies make a terrific salsa, and this dish works well as a taco or burrito filling, or just served over rice and beans.

PREP TIME: 15 minutes
COOKING TIME: 3 hours on high or 5–6 hours on low
ADDITIONAL STEPS: Add cilantro in the last hour of cooking

INGREDIENTS

- **3 pounds (1365 g) boneless, skinless chicken breasts**

- **2 (10-ounce 285-ml) cans salsa verde**

- **1 bunch fresh cilantro, divided**

Cut the chicken into 1- to 2-inch (2.5- to 5-cm) pieces and put into the slow cooker. Add the salsa verde. Cook for 2 hours on high or 4 to 5 hours on low. Rinse the cilantro and remove the leaves, discarding the stems. Chop coarsely. Add half the cilantro to the slow cooker and stir in. Cook for another hour and serve with the remaining fresh cilantro sprinkled over each serving.

YIELD: *4 to 6 servings*

NUTRITIONAL ANALYSIS

301 calories; 6g fat (18.9% calories from fat); 51 g protein; 7g carbohydrate; trace dietary fiber; 138mg cholesterol; 430mg sodium.

Chicken Korma with Chickpeas

This is a much-beloved Indian curried chicken dish. Spice it up with some extra hot pepper, if you wish. It's perfect served over basmati rice with all of those great chutneys, raitas, and pickles that make Indian food so special. (Many of those are available prepared at specialty food stores.)

PREP TIME: 20 minutes
COOKING TIME: 2–3 hours on high or 5–6 hours on low

INGREDIENTS

- **2 pounds (910 g) boneless, skinless chicken breasts**

- **1 (14-ounce or 395-g) can chickpeas**

- **1 (11-ounce or 320-ml) jar korma sauce**

Cut the chicken into 1- to 2-inch (2.5- to 5-cm) pieces and add to the slow cooker. Drain the chickpeas and add to the chicken. Add the korma sauce and stir to combine. Cook for 2 to 3 hours on high or 5 to 6 hours on low.

YIELD: *4 servings*

NUTRITIONAL ANALYSIS

735 calories; 20g fat (24.2% calories from fat); 72g protein; 67g carbohydrate; 19g dietary fiber; 138mg cholesterol; 534mg sodium.

 # Chicken with Fennel

We like this dish because it's a step above the everyday meal, but it's still a snap to make. Slow-cooked fennel develops a sweet flavor and velvety texture that is divine.

PREP TIME: 30 minutes
COOKING TIME: 3 hours on high or 5–6 hours on low
ADDITIONAL STEPS: Brown the chicken pieces before adding to the slow cooker

INGREDIENTS

- **1 fryer chicken, cut up into 8 pieces, or 8 to 10 chicken pieces (about 4 pounds or 1820 g)**

- Salt and pepper to taste

- Cooking oil

- **2 fennel bulbs**

- **1 cup (235 ml) white wine**

Season the chicken pieces with salt and pepper. Heat a large sauté pan over medium-high heat and add a couple of tablespoons (30 ml) of oil. Sear the chicken on all sides to brown well, cooking in batches, if needed, to avoid crowding the pieces.

Remove the tops from the fennel bulbs and discard. Trim away any brown or damaged outer parts of the fennel bulb and cut in half lengthwise. Cut out the core and slice the fennel about ¹/₂ inch (1 cm) thick.

Put the fennel into the slow cooker. Add the seared chicken to the slow cooker. Add the white wine. Cook for 3 hours on high or 5 to 6 hours on low. Serve pieces of chicken with some of the fennel and pan sauce.

YIELD: *4 to 6 servings*

NUTRITIONAL ANALYSIS

587 calories; 39g fat (63.6% calories from fat); 44g protein; 6g carbohydrate; 2g dietary fiber; 226mg cholesterol; 216mg sodium.

Chicken with Mushrooms and Tarragon

These classic flavors blend together into a harmonious whole. Tarragon is an essential herb in French cooking, and it is one of our favorites as well.

PREP TIME: 30 minutes
COOKING TIME: 3 hours on high or 5–6 hours on low
ADDITIONAL STEPS: Sear the chicken breasts before adding to the slow cooker

INGREDIENTS

- **4 chicken breasts, bone-in and skin on (about 2¹⁄₂ pounds or 1140 g)**

- Salt and pepper to taste

- Cooking oil

- **8 ounces (225 g) small white (button) mushrooms**

- **¹⁄₂ cup (32 g) fresh tarragon leaves**

Season the chicken breasts with salt and pepper. Heat a large sauté pan over medium-high heat and add a couple of tablespoons (30 ml) of oil. Sear the chicken, skin side down, until well browned. Turn and brown the other side. Put the chicken into the slow cooker and add the mushrooms, the tarragon, and salt and pepper to taste. Add ¹⁄₂ cup (120 ml) water. Cook for 3 hours on high or 5 to 6 hours on low. Serve the chicken with some of the mushrooms, tarragon leaves, and pan juices.

YIELD: *4 servings*

NUTRITIONAL ANALYSIS

402 calories; 21 g fat (48.6% calories from fat); 48g protein; 2g carbohydrate; 0g dietary fiber; 145mg cholesterol; 318mg sodium.

✚ ADD IT IN!

Substitute white wine for the water.

Chicken with Red Beans and Rice

Nutritious and delicious, this easy meal is sure to be a family favorite.

PREP TIME: 20 minutes

COOKING TIME: 3 hours on high or 5–6 hours on low

INGREDIENTS

- **2 pounds (910 g) boneless, skinless chicken breasts**

- **1 (12-ounce or 340-g) package red beans and rice mix**

- **4 cups (940 ml) chicken broth**

Cut the chicken breasts into 1- to 2-inch (2.5- to 5-cm) pieces and put into the slow cooker. Add the rice and beans and the flavoring package. Add the broth and stir. Cook on high for 3 hours or on low for 5 to 6 hours. The dish is finished when the rice and beans are tender and the stock is fully absorbed.

YIELD: *4 servings*

NUTRITIONAL ANALYSIS

603 calories; 8g fat (12.1 % calories from fat); 68g protein; 60g carbohydrate; 11 g dietary fiber; 138mg cholesterol; 896mg sodium.

Coq au Vin

Simple and classic, this French favorite is sure to please your crowd. Feel free to use whatever combination of chicken parts you prefer, rather than cutting up a full bird.

PREP TIME: 45 minutes

COOKING TIME: 2–3 hours on high or 5–6 hours on low

ADDITIONAL STEPS: Sear the chicken pieces before adding to the slow cooker

+ ADD IT IN!

Add 1 cup (80 g) chopped, cooked bacon in the last hour of cooking, and a handful of chopped fresh thyme to the pot at the beginning.

INGREDIENTS

- **1 fryer chicken, cut up into 8 pieces, or 8 to 10 chicken pieces (about 4 pounds or 1820 g)**

- Salt and pepper to taste

- Cooking oil

- **1 cup (235 ml) red wine**

- **1 (10-ounce or 280-g) bag frozen pearl onions, thawed**

Season the chicken pieces with salt and pepper. Heat a large sauté pan over medium-high heat and add a couple of tablespoons (30 ml) of oil. Sear the chicken on all sides to brown well, cooking in batches, if needed, to avoid crowding the pieces.

Put the seared chicken into the slow cooker and pour the wine over it. Add the pearl onions. Cook for 2 to 3 hours on high or 5 to 6 hours on low. Serve in shallow bowls to allow you to serve some of the pan juices with the chicken and onions.

YIELD: *4 to 6 servings*

NUTRITIONAL ANALYSIS

577 calories; 39g fat (64.9% calories from fat); 43g protein; 4g carbohydrate; 1g dietary fiber; 226mg cholesterol; 312mg sodium.

 # Drumsticks with Hoisin and Honey

Sweet, sassy, and sticky—that's good chicken, and this is a kid favorite. The charter members of our local Suspicious Food Patrol scarfed these down and yelled for more. We were happy to oblige!

PREP TIME: 45 minutes

COOKING TIME: 2–3 hours on high or 4–5 hours on low

ADDITIONAL STEPS: Pre-broil the chicken

INGREDIENTS

- **2 pounds (910 g) chicken drumsticks**

- **1 cup (250 g) hoisin sauce**

- **½ cup (170 g) honey**

Preheat the broiler. Put the drumsticks on a broiler pan and cook for 10 to 12 minutes, until the skin is crisp and brown. Mix together the hoisin sauce and the honey in a large bowl. Add the drumsticks and stir gently to coat. Put the drumsticks in the slow cooker. Cook for 2 to 3 hours on high or 4 to 5 hours on low.

YIELD: *4 servings*

NUTRITIONAL ANALYSIS

579 calories; 22g fat (34.4% calories from fat); 32g protein; 63g carbohydrate; 2g dietary fiber; 139mg cholesterol; 1166mg sodium.

Hearty Chicken Stew

This recipe is great served over biscuits, rice, or mashed potatoes.

PREP TIME: 20 minutes

COOKING TIME: 2–3 hours on high or 5–6 hours on low

INGREDIENTS

- **2 pounds (910 g) boneless, skinless chicken breasts**

- **1 (16-ounce or 475-ml) jar chicken gravy**

- **1 (16-ounce or 455-g) bag frozen mixed vegetables**

Cut the chicken into 1- to 2-inch (2.5- to 5-cm) pieces. Put the chicken into the slow cooker and add the gravy and vegetables. Cook for 2 to 3 hours on high or 5 to 6 hours on low. Stir well before serving.

YIELD: *4 to 6 servings*

NUTRITIONAL ANALYSIS

287 calories; 9g fat (27.2% calories from fat); 38g protein; 14g carbohydrate; 4g dietary fiber; 94mg cholesterol; 552mg sodium.

Lemon Rosemary "Roast" Chicken

A fast sear to brown the skin followed by a slow and gentle cooking makes for a tender, moist, and flavorful roast chicken.

PREP TIME: 30 minutes

COOKING TIME: 3–4 hours on high or 6–7 hours on low

ADDITIONAL STEPS: Sear the chicken to brown the skin before adding to the slow cooker

INGREDIENTS

- **1 roasting chicken (about 4 pounds or 1820 g)**

- Salt and pepper to taste

- Cooking oil

- **2 lemons**

- **4 tablespoons (7 g) chopped fresh rosemary, divided**

+ ADD IT IN!

The pan juices can be made into a gravy by degreasing and stirring in a couple of tablespoons (15 g) of flour mixed in water. Cook over medium-high heat, whisking occasionally, until the gravy boils and thickens.

Rinse the chicken and pat dry inside and out. Salt and pepper the chicken inside the cavity and on the outside. Heat a sauté pan over medium-high heat and add a couple of tablespoons (30 ml) of oil. Sear the chicken, with one side of the breast facing down, for 5 to 8 minutes, then turn and sear the other side for 5 to 8 minutes.

Cut the lemons in half and squeeze the juice into a bowl. Put the lemon halves into the cavity, along with half of the rosemary. Truss the chicken and put it into the slow cooker. Pour the lemon juice over the chicken and sprinkle with the remaining rosemary. Cook for 3 to 4 hours on high or 6 to 7 hours on low. Remove the chicken from the slow cooker and carve.

YIELD: *4 to 6 servings*

NUTRITIONAL ANALYSIS

541 calories; 39g fat (65.7% calories from fat); 43g protein; 3g carbohydrate; trace dietary fiber; 226mg cholesterol; 174mg sodium.

Moroccan Chicken Tagine

A tagine is a Moroccan stew. There are as many variations as there are grains of sand in the Sahara. (Although we might be exaggerating slightly here, there really are a lot.) This simple version is a pleasure served with steamed couscous.

A note on ingredients: Preserved lemons are available at specialty stores and from several online vendors. You can also make your own, but plan on starting them a couple of months prior to making this dish. Do use good imported olives, not the canned American kind.

PREP TIME: 45 minutes

COOKING TIME: 3 hours on high or 5–6 hours on low

ADDITIONAL STEPS: Brown the chicken before adding to the slow cooker

✚ ADD IT IN!

You can add all manner of spices to this dish, particularly cinnamon (sticks are best), saffron, cumin, and coriander.

INGREDIENTS

- **1 fryer chicken, cut up into 8 pieces, or 8 to 10 chicken pieces (about 4 pounds or 1820 g)**
- **Salt and pepper to taste**
- Cooking oil
- **3 small preserved lemons**
- **2 cups (200 g) mixed olives**

Season the chicken pieces with salt and pepper. Heat a large sauté pan over medium-high heat and add a couple of tablespoons (30 ml) of oil. Sear the chicken on all sides to brown well, cooking in batches, if needed, to avoid crowding the pieces.

Put the chicken into the slow cooker. Chop the preserved lemons into small pieces and add to the cooker. Add the olives and ¹/₂ cup (120 ml) water. Cook for 3 hours on high or 5 to 6 hours on low. Serve the chicken pieces with some of the olives, lemon pieces, and pan juices.

YIELD: *4 to 6 servings*

NUTRITIONAL ANALYSIS

606 calories; 44g fat (63.9% calories from fat); 44g protein; 12g carbohydrate; 2g dietary fiber; 226mg cholesterol; 1274mg sodium.

 # Poached Stuffed Chicken Breast

Slice and serve this chicken breast fanned out over scalloped potatoes for an elegant feast.

PREP TIME: 45 minutes

COOKING TIME: 2 hours on high or 4–5 hours on low

ADDITIONAL STEPS: Prepare the stuffing; prepare and roll up the chicken

ADDITIONAL MATERIALS

- Cheesecloth
- Butcher twine

INGREDIENTS

- **1 (10-ounce or 280-g) package stovetop stuffing mix**

- **4 boneless, skinless chicken breasts (about 2 pounds or 910 g)**

- Salt and pepper to taste

- **4 cups (940 ml) chicken broth**

Make the stuffing mix according to package directions and let cool. Meanwhile, put the chicken breasts between 2 sheets of plastic wrap and pound gently with the side of a cleaver or mallet until they are a uniform thickness, about 1/2 inch (1 cm) thick.

Season the chicken with salt and pepper and spoon 1/2 cup (85 g) or so of the stuffing onto each. Tuck in the ends and roll the breasts up to encase the stuffing. Roll the stuffed breasts in cheesecloth and tie the ends of the cloth with butcher twine.

Put the breasts into the slow cooker and add the broth. Cook for 2 hours on high or 4 to 5 hours on low. Remove the chicken from the slow cooker and remove the cheesecloth. Slice each breast into 4 or 5 rounds.

YIELD: *4 servings*

NUTRITIONAL ANALYSIS

580 calories; 10g fat (15.6% calories from fat); 63g protein; 55g carbohydrate; 2g dietary fiber; 139mg cholesterol; 201 0mg sodium.

Roast Chicken and Garlic

We are very enthusiastic about garlic, and this dish is no exception. The key to this recipe is vast quantities of those stinky but delicious little cloves.

PREP TIME: 30 minutes

COOKING TIME: 3–4 hours on high or 6–7 hours on low

ADDITIONAL STEPS: Sear the chicken to brown the skin before adding to the slow cooker

INGREDIENTS

- **1 roasting chicken (about 4 pounds or 1820 g)**

- Salt and pepper to taste

- Cooking oil

- **40 to 50 cloves garlic, peeled, divided**

- **¼ cup (60 ml) soy sauce**

Rinse the chicken and pat dry inside and out. Salt and pepper the chicken inside the cavity and on the outside. Heat a sauté pan over medium-high heat and add a couple tablespoons (30 ml) of oil. Sear the chicken, with one side of the breast facing down, for 5 to 8 minutes, then turn and sear the other side for 5 to 8 minutes.

Put 15 or so cloves of garlic inside the cavity of the chicken. Truss the chicken and put it into the slow cooker. Pour the soy sauce over the chicken and sprinkle the remaining 25 to 35 cloves of garlic around. Cook for 3 to 4 hours on high or 6 to 7 hours on low. Remove the chicken from the slow cooker and carve. Serve with some of the roasted garlic.

YIELD: *4 to 6 servings*

NUTRITIONAL ANALYSIS

579 calories; 39g fat (61.6% calories from fat); 45g protein; 9g carbohydrate; 1g dietary fiber; 226mg cholesterol; 864mg sodium.

# Orange Chicken Breasts

Sweet and tangy at the same time, these citrusy chicken breasts are great with a loaf of crusty bread and a crisp, tossed salad.

PREP TIME: 30 minutes

COOKING TIME: 3 hours on high or 5–6 hours on low

ADDITIONAL STEPS: Sear the chicken before adding to the slow cooker; degrease the sauce; stir in the sour cream just before serving

INGREDIENTS

- **4 chicken breasts, bone-in and skin on (about 2$\frac{1}{2}$ pounds or 1140 g)**

- Salt and pepper to taste

- Cooking oil

- **$\frac{1}{2}$ cup (140 g) orange juice concentrate**

- **1 cup (230 g) sour cream**

Season the chicken breasts with salt and pepper. Heat a large sauté pan over medium-high heat and add a couple of tablespoons (30 ml) of oil. Sear the chicken, skin side down, until well browned. Turn and brown the other side. Put the chicken breasts into the slow cooker and add the orange juice concentrate. (Don't dilute it with water—we want the full-bore concentrate treatment here.) Cook for 3 hours on high or 5 to 6 hours on low. Remove the chicken and keep it warm. Degrease the sauce with a ladle and stir the sour cream into the sauce. Serve each chicken breast with some of the sauce poured over the top.

YIELD: *4 servings*

NUTRITIONAL ANALYSIS

570 calories; 33g fat (53.0% calories from fat); 50g protein; 16g carbohydrate; trace dietary fiber; 171mg cholesterol; 175mg sodium.

Sort of Jambalaya

Any self-respecting Cajun cook would not approve of this recipe, and we do admit that this is a vastly simplified version of that complex dish. The bottom line is, though, that it tastes great and is really easy to make.

PREP TIME: 20 minutes
COOKING TIME: 3 hours on high or 5–6 hours on low

INGREDIENTS

- **2 pounds (910 g) boneless, skinless chicken breasts**

- **1 1/2 cups (290 g) converted rice**

- **2 cups (500 g) marinara sauce with sausage**

- Salt and pepper to taste

Cut the chicken into 1- to 2-inch (2.5- to 5-cm) pieces. Put the chicken, the rice, and the marinara sauce into the slow cooker. Add 1 cup (235 ml) water. Season with salt and pepper to taste. Stir well to coat the rice. Cook for 3 hours on high or 5 to 6 hours on low, until the rice is tender and all of the water is absorbed.

YIELD: *4 servings*

NUTRITIONAL ANALYSIS

712 calories; 20g fat (25.7% calories from fat); 62g protein; 68g carbohydrate; 2g dietary fiber; 158mg cholesterol; 824mg sodium.

✚ ADD IT IN!

Chopped onion and garlic, celery chunks, chopped green peppers, and chopped andouille sausage—all would make this dish even more delicious.

Szechuan Chicken Stew

Spice up a boring weekday with this fabulous stew.

PREP TIME: 20 minutes

COOKING TIME: 2 hours on high or 3–4 hours on low

ADDITIONAL STEPS: Precook the vegetables

INGREDIENTS

- 1 (1-pound or 455-g) bag frozen Szechuan vegetable blend

- 2 pounds (910 g) boneless, skinless chicken breasts

- 1 (12-ounce or 355-ml) bottle Szechuan cooking sauce

Put the vegetables into a saucepan and add 1 cup (235 ml) water. Cook over high heat until boiling. Cook for 2 to 3 minutes and drain well. Put the vegetables into the slow cooker.

Cut the chicken into 1- to 2-inch (2.5- to 5-cm) pieces and add to the slow cooker. Add the Szechuan cooking sauce. Cook for 2 hours on high or 3 to 4 hours on low.

YIELD: *4 to 6 servings*

NUTRITIONAL ANALYSIS

253 calories; 4g fat (15.0% calories from fat); 35g protein; 15g carbohydrate; 2g dietary fiber; 92mg cholesterol; 1795mg sodium.

 Turkey Tortilla Pie

This is a great way to use up leftovers from a holiday meal. It can also be made with cooked chicken meat, so why wait for a holiday?

PREP TIME: 30 minutes
COOKING TIME: 2 hours on high or 4 hours on low

INGREDIENTS

- **4 cups (560 g) cooked, cubed, boneless turkey meat, divided**

- **4 cups (900 g) salsa, divided**

- **12 (8-inch or 20-cm) corn tortillas, divided**

Spread 1 cup (140 g) of turkey in the slow cooker. Top with 1 cup (225 g) of salsa, then top that with 4 tortillas, arranged to fill the circumference of the slow cooker. Repeat the layers twice more, finishing with the remaining 1 cup (140 g) of turkey and 1 cup (225 g) of salsa. Cook for 2 hours on high or 4 hours on low.

YIELD: *4 servings*

NUTRITIONAL ANALYSIS

504 calories; 13g fat (22.6% calories from fat); 48g protein; 51 g carbohydrate; 8g dietary fiber; 104mg cholesterol; 1333mg sodium.

✚ ADD IT IN!

Add 2 cups (230 g) shredded Monterey Jack or cheddar cheese, divided among the layers.

CHAPTER 5

BEEF, VEAL, AND LAMB

What's better than a tender, flavorful roast? Coming home to one that's all ready to eat! Slow cookers are the ultimate tool for creating delicious meat dishes and hearty stews. Even better, they are at their finest with the tougher, less expensive cuts of meat, where the slow, gentle heat creates a dish that's so tender it will fall off the bone. As a bonus, as the seasonings mix with pan juices, many of these dishes create a sauce right along with the roast. For example, the Sweet and Spicy German-Style Pot Roast (page 108) has a perfect gravy ready to pour. Many of the other dishes, such as the Orange-Onion Pot Roast (page 95), build in a side dish that's ready to serve with the main meal, making it even simpler to put a delicious, nutritious meal on the table without undue stress or strain.

 Beef and Noodle Bake

This cozy dinner may be straight out of the Richie and Fonzie Time Capsule, but it's still delicious.

PREP TIME: 25 minutes

COOKING TIME: 3 hours

ADDITIONAL STEPS: Half-cook the noodles and add them to the slow cooker in the last hour

INGREDIENTS

- **2 pounds (910 g) ground beef**

- **2 (12-ounce or 340-g) cans diced tomatoes with onion**

- **1 pound (455 g) egg noodles**

Break up the ground beef into the slow cooker. Add the diced tomatoes and cook on high for 1 hour. Stir to break up the meat into very small bits. Cook for another hour.

Bring a large pot of salted water to a boil and add the egg noodles. Cook for half the recommended time on the package—about 6 minutes. Drain the noodles well and add them to the slow cooker. Stir the noodles and the beef mixture together. Cook for another hour.

YIELD: *6 to 8 servings*

NUTRITIONAL ANALYSIS

586 calories; 33g fat (50.7% calories from fat); 28g protein; 44g carbohydrate; 2g dietary fiber; 150mg cholesterol; 97mg sodium.

➕ ADD IT IN!

Stir ²/₃ cup (80 g) grated cheddar cheese into the mixture.

Beef Braised in Red Wine

We could always tell when our mother was attempting something a little more gourmet than usual, because she cooked with wine. And we responded with whine. Now, of course, we think something like this is terrific comfort food.

PREP TIME: 10 minutes

COOKING TIME: 8 hours

ADDITIONAL STEPS: Reduce the cooking juices to make a sauce

INGREDIENTS

- **1 beef pot roast, such as chuck eye (3 to 4 pounds or 1365 to 1820 g)**

- Salt and pepper to taste

- **2 cups (470 ml) red wine**

- **6 or 7 cloves garlic, peeled**

Put the beef into the slow cooker. Season with salt and pepper. Add the red wine and the garlic. Cook for about 8 hours on low. Remove the beef from the cooker and keep it warm. Degrease the cooking juices and put them into a saucepan. Reduce the juices over high heat until you have about 1$\frac{1}{2}$ cups (355 ml). Slice the beef thin and serve moistened with some of the reduced pan juices.

YIELD: *4 to 6 servings*

NUTRITIONAL ANALYSIS

837 calories; 57g fat (61.8% calories from fat); 75g protein; 5g carbohydrate; trace dietary fiber; 256mg cholesterol; 161mg sodium.

Belgian Beef Stew

This recipe is a riff on Beef Carbonnade, a classic Belgian stew traditionally served with steamed or boiled, buttered potatoes. Use a bottle of good Belgian ale for a full, rich flavor. Like most stew recipes in this book, low and slow is the key. A high temperature results in tough meat.

PREP TIME: 10 minutes
COOKING TIME: 7–8 hours

INGREDIENTS

- **3 pounds (1365 g) stew meat**

- **2 (12-ounce or 355-ml) jars onion gravy**

- **1 (12-ounce or 355-ml) bottle beer**

- Salt and pepper to taste

Place the stew meat into the slow cooker. Add the gravy and beer. Cook on low for 7 to 8 hours. Adjust the seasoning with salt and pepper.

This stew is even better done a day ahead and then reheated for 1 to 2 hours on low.

YIELD: *4 to 6 servings*

NUTRITIONAL ANALYSIS

749 calories; 47g fat (59.1 % calories from fat); 64g protein; 9g carbohydrate; 11 g dietary fiber; 227mg cholesterol; 1109mg sodium.

+ ADD IT IN!

Peel and slice 4 or 5 onions and layer them under the beef. Stir in 1 tablespoon (15 g) strong mustard for a tad more zest.

Braised Beef Brisket

This dish is the tender and flavorful pot roast of your dreams! You can substitute another cut of beef for the brisket, such as chuck eye. You can also sear the beef before adding it to the slow cooker, if you wish.

PREP TIME: 10 minutes

COOKING TIME: 7–8 hours

ADDITIONAL STEPS: Reduce the cooking juices to make a sauce

INGREDIENTS

- **1 beef brisket, flat cut (about 4 pounds or 1820 g)**

- Salt and pepper to taste

- **1 cup (235 ml) red wine**

- **1 cup (250 g) mushroom marinara sauce**

Put the brisket into the slow cooker and sprinkle with salt and pepper. Pour the wine and tomato sauce over. Cook on low for 7 to 8 hours.

Remove the beef from the slow cooker and keep it warm. Degrease the pan juices and reduce them to about 1½ cups (355 ml) in a saucepan over medium-high heat. Serve the beef sliced with some of the gravy.

YIELD: *4 to 6 servings*

NUTRITIONAL ANALYSIS

1112 calories; 84g fat (70.4% calories from fat); 57g protein; 23g carbohydrate; 0g dietary fiber; 221 mg cholesterol; 2711mg sodium.

 ADD IT IN!

Peel and mince 3 or 4 cloves of garlic and add them to the mixture.

Braised Lamb Shoulder Chops

This dish is typical French-country-style cooking at its best. The white beans are a delightfully different twist from our usual fare.

PREP TIME: 20 minutes

COOKING TIME: 2 hours

ADDITIONAL STEPS: Brown the chops before adding them to the slow cooker

INGREDIENTS

- **4 lamb shoulder chops (about 21/2 pounds or 1140 g)**

- Salt and pepper to taste

- **1 (22-ounce or 615-g) can white beans, drained**

- **1 (12-ounce or 340-g) can diced tomatoes with red wine and herbs**

Heat a sauté pan over medium-high heat. Season the chops with salt and pepper and sear in the pan until browned on both sides, cooking in batches, if needed. Put the lamb chops into the slow cooker and add the drained beans and diced tomatoes. Cook on high for 2 hours. Serve some of the beans and sauce with each chop.

YIELD: *4 servings*

NUTRITIONAL ANALYSIS

495 calories; 26g fat (47.1% calories from fat); 28g protein; 38g carbohydrate; 8g dietary fiber; 70mg cholesterol; 69mg sodium.

✚ ADD IT IN!

Deepen the flavor of the sauce by adding several cloves of chopped garlic and 1/2 cup (120 ml) red wine.

Corned Beef and Cabbage

*Here's a no-muss, no-fuss way to make your St. Patrick's Day favorite.
(Leprechauns and shamrocks not included.)*

PREP TIME: 20 minutes
COOKING TIME: 8–9 hours
ADDITIONAL STEPS: Add the cabbage and potatoes in the last 2–3 hours

INGREDIENTS

- **1 corned beef (about 4 pounds or 1820 g)**

- **1 small head green cabbage (about 2 pounds or 910 g)**

- **6 medium boiling potatoes (about 2 pounds or 910 g)**

Put the corned beef and any spice package that comes with it into the slow cooker. Add water to barely cover the meat. Cook on low for 6 hours.

Cut the cabbage into 6 wedges. Peel the potatoes. Add the vegetables to the slow cooker and cook for 2 to 3 hours more.

Remove the corned beef from the cooker. Slice it thin. Remove the cabbage and potatoes from the pot and allow the cabbage to drain. Serve slices of corned beef with a piece of the cabbage and a potato.

YIELD: *6 servings*

NUTRITIONAL ANALYSIS

693 calories; 45g fat (59.1% calories from fat); 47g protein; 23g carbohydrate; 2g dietary fiber; 162mg cholesterol; 375mg sodium.

 ADD IT IN!

We like to pour a little malt vinegar over our cabbage for a zesty kick.

 Cheesesteaks

Just add sub rolls for a great game-day feast!

PREP TIME: 20 minutes

COOKING TIME: 3 hours

ADDITIONAL STEPS: Add the cheese in the last hour

INGREDIENTS

- **4 medium-size onions**

- **2 pounds (910 g) shaved sandwich steak**

- Salt and pepper to taste

- **1 pound (455 g) processed cheese, such as Velveeta**

Peel and slice the onions. Break the onion rounds into rings and put them into the slow cooker. Add the steak and season with salt and pepper. Cook for 2 hours on high. Add the cheese and cook for another hour on low. Stir until the cheese is smooth.

YIELD: *6 to 8 servings*

NUTRITIONAL ANALYSIS

590 calories; 43g fat (64.1% calories from fat); 39g protein; 15g carbohydrate; 1g dietary fiber; 147mg cholesterol; 1519mg sodium.

 Meatloaf

Serve this with baked potatoes and green beans—June Cleaver would be proud!

PREP TIME: 20 minutes

COOKING TIME: 3 hours on high or 6 hours on low

INGREDIENTS

- **2 pounds (910 g) lean ground beef**

- **3 eggs**

- **2 cups (230 g) seasoned bread crumbs**

- Salt and pepper to taste

In a large bowl, mix together the ground beef, eggs, bread crumbs, and salt and pepper to taste. Put the meat mixture into the slow cooker and pat it lightly into the shape you wish. You can make a loaf in the slow cooker, or pat it out until the meat fills the bottom to the edges. Cook on high for 3 hours or on low for 6 hours.

YIELD: *6 servings*

NUTRITIONAL ANALYSIS

644 calories; 44g fat (62.9% calories from fat); 32g protein; 26g carbohydrate; 1g dietary fiber; 222mg cholesterol; 441 mg sodium.

✚ ADD IT IN!

We've been known to shake a couple of teaspoons of Bell's Seasoning into our meatloaf mixture.

 Dry Rub Slow-Cooked Beef Ribs

Look for the meatiest beef ribs you can find. There are many varieties of dry rubs on the market, so use your favorite.

PREP TIME: 15 minutes
COOKING TIME: 8 hours

INGREDIENTS

- **3 to 4 pounds (1365 to 1820 g) beef back ribs**

- **1 cup (100 g) beef steak/BBQ rub**

- **4 medium-size onions**

Cut the beef into individual ribs. Toss the ribs in a large bowl with the rub until the meat is well coated. Peel the onions and cut them into thin slices. Put the onions into the slow cooker and add the ribs. Cook on low for 8 hours. Serve the ribs with some of the onions, if desired.

YIELD: *4 servings*

NUTRITIONAL ANALYSIS

Per Serving (not including BBQ rub, which varies a lot): 1463 calories; 123g fat (76.4% calories from fat); 76g protein; 9g carbohydrate; 2g dietary fiber; 322mg cholesterol; 248mg sodium.

Easy All-Day Spaghetti Sauce

This slow-cooked, rich, and delicious sauce is perfect over any pasta.

PREP TIME: 10 minutes

COOKING TIME: 6–7 hours

ADDITIONAL STEPS: Stir to break up the beef after 2 hours

INGREDIENTS

- **1 pound (455 g) ground beef**

- **3 (12-ounce or 340-g) cans diced tomato with garlic and onion**

- **1/2 cup (120 ml) red wine**

Break up the ground beef into the slow cooker. Puree 1 of the cans of diced tomatoes in a food processor or blender. Add all 3 cans of tomatoes and the red wine to the slow cooker. Cook on high for 2 hours. Stir to break up the beef into very small pieces. Turn the cooker to low and cook for 4 to 5 hours more.

YIELD: *4 to 6 servings over pasta*

NUTRITIONAL ANALYSIS

284 calories; 21 g fat (67.6% calories from fat); 14g protein; 8g carbohydrate; 2g dietary fiber; 64mg cholesterol; 80mg sodium.

✚ ADD IT IN!

Slice and dice 1 small onion, chop some fresh basil, and add them to the slow cooker.

 Fast Then Slow Beef Stew

The fast part is the preparation; the slow part, the gentle cooking. The result is tender meat and a delicious stew.

PREP TIME: 15 minutes
COOKING TIME: 7–8 hours

INGREDIENTS

- **2 pounds (910 g) stew beef**

- **3 pounds (1365 g) potatoes**

- **2 (12-ounce or 355-ml) cans onion gravy**

- Salt and pepper to taste

Put the stew beef into the slow cooker. Peel the potatoes and cut them into 1- to 2-inch (2.5- to 5-cm) chunks. Add the potatoes to the cooker. Add the gravy. Cook on low for 7 to 8 hours. Adjust the seasoning to taste.

YIELD: *6 to 8 servings*

NUTRITIONAL ANALYSIS

506 calories; 24g fat (42.8% calories from fat); 36g protein; 36g carbohydrate; 11g dietary fiber; 113mg cholesterol; 673mg sodium.

 ADD IT IN!

We like to add 2 or 3 handfuls of baby carrots to the stew as well.

Lamb Shanks with Lentils

Most folks tend to relegate lentils to the sproutsy crowd, and that's a shame. These cousins of beans and peas are packed with protein, are rich in iron, and contain folic acid. Moreover, they are a classic item in French cooking, as this delicious dish attests.

PREP TIME: 10 minutes

COOKING TIME: 8 hours

ADDITIONAL STEPS: Brown the lamb shanks before adding them to the slow cooker; deglaze the sauté pan; check after 4 hours

INGREDIENTS

- **2 cups (400 g) lentils, picked over and rinsed**

- **4 lamb shanks (about 3 pounds or 1365 g)**

- Salt and pepper to taste

- Cooking oil

- **2 cups (470 ml) red wine**

 ADD IT IN!
Several peeled garlic cloves added to the slow cooker will give this dish a definite kick.

Put the lentils into the slow cooker. Season the lamb shanks with salt and pepper. Heat a sauté pan over medium-high heat and add a couple of tablespoons (30 ml) of oil. Sear the shanks, in batches if necessary, to brown on all sides. Put the shanks into the slow cooker. Deglaze the sauté pan with the red wine and add to the slow cooker. Add 1 cup (235 ml) water to the cooker. Cook for 8 hours on low. Check after 4 hours or so and add more water, if needed.

YIELD: *4 servings*

NUTRITIONAL ANALYSIS

957 calories; 38g fat (38.6% calories from fat); 78g protein; 57g carbohydrate; 29g dietary fiber; 182mg cholesterol; 241 mg sodium.

🐄 Orange-Onion Pot Roast

Here's a classic pot roast with a twist. Beef and orange are great flavor buddies, and the onions make a tasty accompaniment.

PREP TIME: 20 minutes
COOKING TIME: 8 hours
ADDITIONAL STEPS: Brown the pot roast before adding it to the slow cooker; degrease the pan juices

INGREDIENTS

- **3 medium-size onions**

- Cooking oil

- **1 beef pot roast (about 3 pounds or 1365 g)**

- Salt and pepper to taste

- **1 cup (320 g) orange marmalade**

Peel the onions and slice thin. Put the onions into the slow cooker. Heat a sauté pan over medium-high heat and add a couple of tablespoons (30 ml) of oil. Season the pot roast with salt and pepper and sear in the sauté pan on all sides to brown. Put the beef into the slow cooker and spread the marmalade over it. Add ½ cup (120 ml) water. Cook on low for 8 hours. Remove the beef from the cooker and slice thin. Degrease the pan juices and serve the beef with some of the onions and pan juices.

YIELD: *4 to 6 servings*

NUTRITIONAL ANALYSIS

625 calories; 35g fat (51.0% calories from fat); 37g protein; 40g carbohydrate; 4g dietary fiber; 131 mg cholesterol; 145mg sodium.

 # Osso Buco

This classic Italian dish is traditionally served with risotto and topped with gremolata, a sprightly garnish made of minced garlic, lemon zest, and parsley.

PREP TIME: 25 minutes

COOKING TIME: 8 hours

ADDITIONAL STEPS: Brown the veal before adding it to the slow cooker

INGREDIENTS

- **4 pounds (1820 g) veal shanks, cut about 2 inches (5 cm) long**

- Salt and pepper to taste

- Cooking oil

- **1 cup (250 g) garlic marinara sauce**

- **¹⁄₂ cup (120 ml) white wine**

Heat a sauté pan over medium-high heat. Season the shanks with salt and pepper. Put a couple of tablespoons (30 ml) of oil into the sauté pan and sear the veal on each side until browned, working in batches, if necessary, to avoid crowding the pan. Put the veal into the slow cooker and add the marinara sauce and wine. Cook for 8 hours on low. Carefully remove the veal from the cooker. Serve the shanks topped with some of the sauce.

YIELD: *4 to 6 servings*

NUTRITIONAL ANALYSIS

391 calories; 10g fat (25.3% calories from fat); 64g protein; 4g carbohydrate; 1g dietary fiber; 236mg cholesterol; 363mg sodium.

✚ ADD IT IN!

Add several handfuls of baby carrots, along with a small, diced onion, to deepen the flavor.

 Pomegranate Lamb

Pomegranate juice continues to be a culinary darling, and with good reason. This combination provides a piquant and delicious meal.

PREP TIME: 30 minutes
COOKING TIME: 6–7 hours

INGREDIENTS

- **3 medium-size onions**

- **1 boneless leg of lamb (about 3 pounds or 1365 g)**

- Salt and pepper to taste

- **1 cup (235 ml) pomegranate juice**

Peel and slice the onions 1/4 inch (6 mm) thick. Break up the onion rings into the slow cooker. Trim as much fat as possible from the lamb and cut the meat into 2-inch (5-cm) chunks. Add to the cooker. Season with salt and pepper to taste and pour the pomegranate juice over the meat. Cook for 6 to 7 hours on low.

YIELD: *6 servings*

NUTRITIONAL ANALYSIS

456 calories; 31 g fat (61.4% calories from fat); 33g protein; 11 g carbohydrate; 1g dietary fiber; 124mg cholesterol; 107mg sodium.

Roast Veal Shoulder

Veal shoulder makes a delicious slow-cooker roast. The bacon adds flavor and needed moisture to this lean meat. You can discard the bacon after cooking, if you wish.

PREP TIME: 10 minutes
COOKING TIME: 6–8 hours

INGREDIENTS

- **1 boneless rolled veal shoulder roast (3 to 4 pounds or 1365 to 1820 g)**

- Salt and pepper to taste

- **4 slices bacon**

- **½ cup (120 ml) white wine**

Put the veal roast into the slow cooker. Season the meat with salt and pepper. Drape the bacon on top of the meat. Pour the wine over all. Cook on low for 6 to 8 hours. Remove the meat from the cooker and remove and discard the bacon. Remove the twine from the roast and slice. The cooking liquid can be reduced to make a simple sauce, or it can be a base for gravy.

YIELD: *6 to 8 servings*

NUTRITIONAL ANALYSIS

265 calories; 11 g fat (41.6% calories from fat); 36g protein; trace carbohydrate; 0g dietary fiber; 150mg cholesterol; 200mg sodium.

 ADD IT IN!

Sprinkle the roast with some chopped fresh rosemary for an added flavor dimension.

Szechuan Beef and Vegetables

It is impossible to stir-fry in a slow cooker, but you can create a tasty, stew-like version of this Chinese dish. Serve over steamed rice.

PREP TIME: 20 minutes

COOKING TIME: 3 hours

ADDITIONAL STEPS: Add the vegetables in the last 1^1/$_2$ hours

INGREDIENTS

- 1 pound (455 g) sirloin, round, or other lean steak

- 1^1/$_2$ cups (355 ml) Szechuan cooking sauce

- 1 (1-pound or 455-g) bag Asian vegetable mix

Trim all the fat and gristle from the steak. Slice the meat into strips measuring about ^{1}/$_2$ inch x 2 inches x 1 inch (1 cm x 5 cm x 2.5 cm). Put the meat into the slow cooker and add the cooking sauce. Cook on high for 1^1/$_2$ hours. While the meat is cooking, defrost the vegetables. Stir the vegetables into the stew and cook for another 1^1/$_2$ hours.

YIELD: *4 servings*

NUTRITIONAL ANALYSIS

396 calories; 19g fat (46.6% calories from fat); 24g protein; 26g carbohydrate; 3g dietary fiber; 78mg cholesterol; 3335mg sodium.

Simple Ground Beef Stroganoff

Serve this luscious stroganoff over rice or egg noodles.

PREP TIME: 10 minutes

COOKING TIME: 2 hours on high or 4 hours on low

ADDITIONAL STEPS: Add sour cream at the end of cooking

INGREDIENTS

- **1 pound (455 g) ground beef**

- **1 (12-ounce or 355-ml) can mushroom gravy**

- **1 cup (230 g) sour cream**

- Salt and pepper to taste

Break up the beef into small pieces and put into the slow cooker. Add the gravy. Cook for 2 hours on high or 4 hours on low. Stir in the sour cream and adjust the seasoning to taste.

YIELD: *4 servings*

NUTRITIONAL ANALYSIS

518 calories; 44g fat (77.6% calories from fat); 22g protein; 7g carbohydrate; trace dietary fiber; 122mg cholesterol; 593mg sodium.

✚ ADD IT IN!

Slice up 10 or so white (button) mushrooms and stir them into the ground beef mixture.

 Simple Veal Stew

This recipe is great as is, or it can be embellished in many ways. Try adding diced carrots, or some tomato, garlic, or fresh herbs. It's great over pasta, polenta, risotto, or mashed potatoes.

PREP TIME: 10 minutes
COOKING TIME: 7–8 hours

INGREDIENTS

- **2 pounds (910 g) stew veal**

- **1 cup (235 ml) red wine**

- **1 (12-ounce or 355-ml) can mushroom gravy**

- Salt and pepper to taste

Put the veal, red wine, and gravy into the slow cooker and stir them together. Season with salt and pepper to taste (remember, the gravy will already add some salt). Cook on low for 7 to 8 hours.

YIELD: *6 to 8 servings over pasta or rice*

NUTRITIONAL ANALYSIS

388 calories; 25g fat (61.3% calories from fat); 32g protein; 3g carbohydrate; trace dietary fiber; 113mg cholesterol; 595mg sodium.

 Rib Roast

Restaurants get their prime rib to stay so juicy and evenly cooked with special roasting ovens that utilize low heat—just like a slow cooker. Small round cooking racks are pretty easy to find, but you can improvise a cooking rack with foil, or with a layer of sliced onions. We recommend using the low setting to reduce shrinkage.

PREP TIME: 10 minutes

COOKING TIME: 2 hours on high or 4–5 hours on low

SPECIAL EQUIPMENT

- Wire rack that fits into the slow cooker

INGREDIENTS

- **1 standing rib roast, bone-in (about 4 pounds or 1820 g)**

- **4 tablespoons (40 g) minced garlic**

- **4 tablespoons (7 g) minced fresh rosemary**

- Salt and pepper to taste

Put the roasting rack into the slow cooker. Place the roast on it, fat side up. Spread the garlic on the meat and sprinkle with the rosemary. Sprinkle generously with salt and pepper. Cook on high for about 2 hours or low for 4 to 5 hours for a medium-rare roast. Allow the roast to stand for 15 to 20 minutes before cutting.

YIELD: *8 to 10 servings*

NUTRITIONAL ANALYSIS

578 calories; 49g fat (77.6% calories from fat); 30g protein; 2g carbohydrate; 1g dietary fiber; 129mg cholesterol; 99mg sodium.

 Taco Filling

This easy recipe is the basis for a great taco feast. These spice mixes are found in most Latin markets.

PREP TIME: 10 minutes

COOKING TIME: 3 hours on high or 5–7 hours on low

ADDITIONAL STEPS: Break up the meat halfway through cooking

INGREDIENTS

- **2 pounds (910 g) ground beef**

- Salt and pepper to taste

- **1 (1-ounce or 30-g) package Menudo or other Mexican spice mix**

- **1 (6-ounce or 175-ml) can tomato sauce**

Break up the beef into small chunks and add to the slow cooker. Season with salt and pepper to taste and add the spice mix. Be sure to crush any large herb leaves with your fingers. Add the tomato sauce. Cook on high for 1½ hours or on low for 3 to 4 hours. Using a slotted spoon, break up the meat until it is in fine pieces. Continue to cook on high for 1½ hours or on low for another 2 to 3 hours.

YIELD: *6 to 8 servings*

NUTRITIONAL ANALYSIS

364 calories; 30g fat (75.5% calories from fat); 19g protein; 3g carbohydrate; 1g dietary fiber; 96mg cholesterol; 207mg sodium.

 # Stewed Beef Short Ribs

Short ribs are a cut of beef that's naturally suited to the slow cooker. Because short ribs are a fatty cut of meat, it's best to cook this recipe ahead, leaving time to degrease the cooking liquid and produce a flavorful sauce.

PREP TIME: 15 minutes

COOKING TIME: 7–8 hours

ADDITIONAL STEPS: Remove the ribs and degrease the sauce

INGREDIENTS

- **3 medium-size onions**

- **3 pounds (1365 g) beef short ribs**

- Salt and pepper to taste

- **1 (12-ounce or 355-ml) jar beef gravy**

Peel and slice the onions thin. Put the onion slices into the slow cooker. Put the short ribs on top of the onions and sprinkle with salt and pepper to taste. Pour the gravy over the ribs. Cook on low for 7 to 8 hours. Remove the ribs from the cooker and keep them warm. Degrease the cooking liquid and put it and the braised onions into a saucepan. Reduce over high heat until you have about 2 cups (470 ml) of liquid. Serve the short ribs with some of the sauce over them.

YIELD: *4 servings*

NUTRITIONAL ANALYSIS

1142 calories; 94g fat (74.8% calories from fat); 60g protein; 11 g carbohydrate; 2g dietary fiber; 244mg cholesterol; 663mg sodium.

 # Stewed Beef with Dried Plums

We are being politically correct here to keep the Dried Plums Council happy, but we all know that these are prunes—a delicious, sweet, and healthy snack that suffers from bad PR. Either way, they are a great match with beef.

PREP TIME: 10 minutes
COOKING TIME: 7–8 hours

INGREDIENTS

- **2 pounds (910 g) stew beef**

- **2 cups (350 g) dried plums (prunes)**

- **1 cup (235 ml) ruby port wine**

- Salt and pepper to taste

Combine the beef, the dried plums, and the port in the slow cooker. Add salt and pepper to taste. Cook on low for 7 to 8 hours.

YIELD: *6 servings*

NUTRITIONAL ANALYSIS

656 calories; 31 g fat (46.0% calories from fat); 43g protein; 40g carbohydrate; 4g dietary fiber; 151mg cholesterol; 448mg sodium.

Stuffed Beef Round Steak

This is a simpler take on the classic Italian dish braciola. The round steak is cut very thin, stuffed, tied, and braised in a flavorful marinara sauce. Slices of meat are served with the cooking sauce. In New England, round steak is often sold thinly cut specifically for this dish. If you can't find it this way at your market, ask the butcher to cut the meat thin for you. We recommend using the low temperature setting for a more tender dish.

PREP TIME: 45 minutes

COOKING TIME: 7–8 hours

ADDITIONAL STEPS: Cook the stuffing; prepare the meat

INGREDIENTS

- **1 (12-ounce or 340-g) package stovetop stuffing mix**

- **1 thin-cut top round steak (about 2 pounds or 910 g)**

- Salt and pepper to taste

- Cooking oil

- **2 cups (490 g) marinara sauce**

ADDITIONAL MATERIALS

- Butcher twine

Prepare the stuffing mix according to package directions and set aside to cool.

Lay the steak on a cutting board and cover with plastic wrap. With the side of a cleaver or with a meat mallet, gently pound the meat to a uniform thickness. Sprinkle with salt and pepper.

Spread the stuffing onto the meat and roll up the meat. Tie the roll with butcher's twine. Heat a sauté pan large enough to hold the steak over medium-high heat. Add a couple of tablespoons (30 ml) of oil and sear the beef on all sides.

Transfer the beef to the slow cooker and add the marinara sauce. Cook for 7 to 8 hours on low. Remove the meat from the slow cooker and remove the twine. Cut rounds about $1/2$ inch (1 cm) thick. Serve with some of the cooking sauce, passing the remaining sauce at the table.

YIELD: *4 to 6 servings*

NUTRITIONAL ANALYSIS

555 calories; 22g fat (36.3% calories from fat); 36g protein; 50g carbohydrate; 3g dietary fiber; 90mg cholesterol; 1320mg sodium.

✚ ADD IT IN!

Feel free to add embellishments on top of the stuffing, such as Italian cold cuts, provolone cheese, or even peeled and sliced hard-boiled eggs laid end to end.

 # Sweet and Spicy German-Style Pot Roast

The gingersnaps in this recipe cook down into a delicious sauce. The smaller members of our food-testing panel generally view any condiments other than ketchup with deep suspicion, but they gobbled up this sauce with shouts of happy glee.

PREP TIME: 10 minutes

COOKING TIME: 8 hours

ADDITIONAL STEPS: Degrease the sauce

INGREDIENTS

- **1 beef pot roast (about 3 pounds or 1365 g)**

- **10 to 12 gingersnaps**

- **¹⁄₂ cup (125 g) steak sauce**

Put the beef into the slow cooker. Crumble the gingersnaps over the beef and pour the steak sauce over all. Cook on low for 8 hours. Remove the beef from the slow cooker and keep it warm. Degrease the cooking liquid and stir until smooth. Slice the beef and serve with some of the sauce over it.

YIELD: *6 servings*

NUTRITIONAL ANALYSIS

543 calories; 37g fat (62.1% calories from fat); 37g protein; 14g carbohydrate; 1g dietary fiber; 131mg cholesterol; 496mg sodium.

 # Swiss Steak

This classic dish is wonderful served with spaetzle, noodles, or boiled potatoes.

PREP TIME: 30 minutes
COOKING TIME: 3 hours on high or 6 hours on low
ADDITIONAL STEPS: Brown the steaks before putting them into the slow cooker

INGREDIENTS

- **2 pounds (910 g) round steak, cut about 1 inch (2.5 cm) thick**

- Salt and pepper to taste

- **1 cup (125 g) all-purpose flour**

- ¼ cup (60 ml) cooking oil

- **1 (12-ounce or 340-g) can diced tomatoes with celery and onion**

Cut the steak into 4 equal-size pieces. Pound the steak lightly with a meat tenderizer. Season with salt and pepper and dredge the meat in the flour. Heat a sauté pan over medium-high heat and add the oil. Sauté the beef until well browned, then turn and repeat on the other side. Put the browned meat into the slow cooker. Add the diced tomatoes and cook for 3 hours on high or 6 hours on low. Serve the steak with some of the sauce over it.

YIELD: *4 servings*

NUTRITIONAL ANALYSIS

685 calories; 42g fat (55.4% calories from fat); 47g protein; 28g carbohydrate; 2g dietary fiber; 134mg cholesterol; 121mg sodium.

CHAPTER 6
PORK

Pork has evolved from something to put next to fried eggs or serve for holidays into an economical meat that rivals chicken in popularity. Pork blends well with so many flavors and complementary foods that it's difficult to find something it clashes with. Today's pork is a far cry from the fatty cuts of previous decades. "The other white meat" is a versatile star that can be substituted for veal or chicken in many dishes. Best of all, it takes well to the low-heat, slow-braising style of the slow cooker.

🐖 Brats in Beer

Bratwurst sausages are a classic barbecue item in the Midwest, and with good reason. Slow cooking helps bring the taste of barbecue indoors.

PREP TIME: 10 minutes

COOKING TIME: 2 hours on high or 4 hours on low

INGREDIENTS

- **1 pound (455 g) bratwursts**

- **1 (12-ounce or 355-ml) can beer**

Put the bratwursts into the slow cooker. Add the beer and enough water to cover the sausages. Cook for 2 hours on high or 4 hours on low.

 SERVING SUGGESTION: *Serve the sausages on rolls.*

YIELD: *4 to 6 servings*

NUTRITIONAL ANALYSIS

251 calories; 20g fat (75.3% calories from fat); 11 g protein; 4g carbohydrate; trace dietary fiber; 45mg cholesterol; 424mg sodium.

Cherry-Glazed Pork Roast

Pork pairs well with so many fruits. Here, we use cherries for a tart and tasty flavor twist.

PREP TIME: 10 minutes
COOKING TIME: 3 hours on high or 6–7 hours on low
ADDITIONAL STEPS: Degrease the pan liquids and make a sauce

INGREDIENTS

- **1 boneless pork loin roast (about 3 pounds or 1365 g)**

- Salt and pepper to taste

- **1 (12-ounce or 340-g) jar cherry preserves**

- **2 tablespoons (30 ml) balsamic vinegar**

- 4 tablespoons ($^1/_2$ stick or 55 g) unsalted butter

Season the roast with salt and pepper and place it in the slow cooker. Spread the cherry preserves over the pork and add $^1/_2$ cup (120 ml) water to the slow cooker. Cook on high for about 2 hours, or for 6 to 7 hours on low, until a meat thermometer inserted into the thickest part reads 165°F. Remove the roast from the cooker and keep it warm. Degrease the pan juices. Put the degreased juice into a saucepan and add the balsamic vinegar. Bring to a boil and reduce to about $^1/_2$ cup (120 ml). Swirl in the butter to make an emulsified sauce. Adjust the salt and pepper to taste. Serve slices of the roast with some of the sauce over it.

YIELD: *6 to 8 servings*

NUTRITIONAL ANALYSIS

321 calories; 22g fat (61.8% calories from fat); 25g protein; 5g carbohydrate; trace dietary fiber; 100mg cholesterol; 137mg sodium.

Chinese-Style Ribs

This is everybody's favorite—tender ribs bathed in the classic red glaze, and without the expense of takeout!

PREP TIME: 20 minutes

COOKING TIME: 4 hours on high or 8–9 hours on low

INGREDIENTS

- **2 racks spareribs (about 4 pounds or 1890 g)**

- Salt and pepper to taste

- **1 (12-ounce or 355-ml) jar Chinese pork glaze**

Cut the ribs into 2 or 3 rib sections. Sprinkle the meat with salt and pepper to taste. Put the ribs into a bowl, add the pork glaze, and toss to coat. Put the ribs into the slow cooker and cook for about 4 hours on high or 8 to 9 hours on low.

YIELD: *4 to 6 servings*

NUTRITIONAL ANALYSIS

757 calories; 44g fat (53.4% calories from fat); 33g protein; 55g carbohydrate; 1g dietary fiber; 146mg cholesterol; 727mg sodium.

Country-Style Pork Ribs with Paprikash Sauce

PREP TIME: 10 minutes

COOKING TIME: 5–6 hours

ADDITIONAL STEPS: Add yogurt to the sauce after cooking

INGREDIENTS

- **2 pounds (910 g) country-style pork ribs**

- **4 tablespoons (30 g) paprika**

- Salt and pepper to taste

- **1 cup (230 g) plain yogurt**

Put the ribs into the slow cooker. Combine the paprika and salt and pepper to taste, then add enough water to make a paste. Rub the paste on the ribs. Add ¹/₂ cup (120 ml) water to the slow cooker and cook the ribs on low for 5 to 6 hours. Remove the ribs from the slow cooker and keep them warm. Put 1 cup (235 ml) of the sauce into a saucepan and bring to a boil. Stir in the yogurt. Serve the ribs with the yogurt sauce.

YIELD: *4 to 6 servings*

NUTRITIONAL ANALYSIS

307 calories; 24g fat (70.6% calories from fat); 18g protein; 4g carbohydrate; 1g dietary fiber; 78mg cholesterol; 92mg sodium.

✚ ADD IT IN!

Add a can of chopped tomatoes with herbs and some chopped celery to deepen the flavor.

🐖 Easy Barbecue Ribs

Fall-off-the-bone tender ribs basted in tangy barbecue sauce, with the added bonus of a side of delicious braised onions. What's not to like?

PREP TIME: 15 minutes
COOKING TIME: 8 hours
ADDITIONAL STEPS: Add more barbecue sauce in the last $1/2$ hour

INGREDIENTS

- **4 medium-size onions**

- **2 racks pork ribs (about 4 pounds or 1820 g)**

- **2 cups (500 g) barbecue sauce (your favorite), divided**

Peel and cut the onions into thin slices. Break the slices into rings and put them into the slow cooker. Cut the ribs into 3 or 4 rib sections and put them into a large bowl. Add 1 cup (250 g) of the barbecue sauce and toss the ribs to coat. Place the ribs on top of the onions. Cook on low for $7 1/2$ hours. Baste the ribs with the remaining 1 cup (250 g) barbecue sauce and cook for another $1/2$ hour. Serve rib portions with some of the braised onions.

YIELD: *4 to 6 servings*

NUTRITIONAL ANALYSIS

627 calories; 46g fat (66.8% calories from fat); 34g protein; 17g carbohydrate; 2g dietary fiber; 146mg cholesterol; 824mg sodium.

Ham and Cabbage Casserole

This would be perfect with some noodles or spaetzle on the side for a nice, cozy winter dinner!

PREP TIME: 30 minutes

COOKING TIME: 2–3 hours on high or 6–7 hours on low

INGREDIENTS

- **1 small head green cabbage**

- **1 pound (455 g) boneless ham, sliced**

- **1 (10-ounce or 285-ml) can condensed cream of cheddar soup**

Core and shred the cabbage and place in alternating layers with the ham slices in the slow cooker. Pour the cream of cheddar soup over all. Cook for 2 to 3 hours on high or 6 to 7 hours on low.

YIELD: *4 to 6 servings*

NUTRITIONAL ANALYSIS

168 calories; 10g fat (54.3% calories from fat); 14g protein; 5g carbohydrate; trace dietary fiber; 49mg cholesterol; 1181 mg sodium.

✚ ADD IT IN!

Layer in some shredded cheddar to intensify the cheese flavor.

 Ham and Potato Bake

Here's a good way to use up that leftover Easter ham.

PREP TIME: 30 minutes

COOKING TIME: 2 hours on high or 4 hours on low

INGREDIENTS

- **4 pounds (1820 g) potatoes**

- **1 pound (455 g) ham, thinly sliced**

- **1 (16-ounce or 475-ml) jar Alfredo sauce**

Peel the potatoes and slice them ¼ inch (6 mm) thick. Put a layer of potatoes in the slow cooker, top with some ham, and repeat until the ingredients are all used, ending with potatoes on top. Pour the Alfredo sauce over all and cook for 4 hours on low or 2 hours on high.

YIELD: *4 to 6 servings*

NUTRITIONAL ANALYSIS

523 calories; 22g fat (36.9% calories from fat); 23g protein; 60g carbohydrate; 5g dietary fiber; 86mg cholesterol; 1417mg sodium.

✚ ADD IT IN!

Sprinkle ½ cup (40 g) of shredded Parmesan cheese on top of the casserole.

Honey and Soy Ribs

Break out the extra napkins—or a roll of paper towels—for these babies.

PREP TIME: 20 minutes
COOKING TIME: 6–8 hours

INGREDIENTS

- **1 rack pork ribs (about 2 pounds or 910 g)**

- **1 cup (340 g) honey**

- **1/2 cup (120 ml) soy sauce**

- Pepper to taste

Cut the ribs into 1 or 2 rib sections. Place the ribs in a large bowl and add the honey, soy sauce, and pepper to taste. Toss to coat the ribs well. Put the ribs into the slow cooker and cook on low for 6 to 8 hours.

YIELD: *2 to 4 servings*

NUTRITIONAL ANALYSIS

679 calories; 33g fat (43.0% calories from fat); 26g protein; 73g carbohydrate; trace dietary fiber; 110mg cholesterol; 2168mg sodium.

Italian Sausage and Peppers

Serve this up on a sub roll or over pasta. You can use red, yellow, or green peppers, or a mixture—whatever you prefer.

PREP TIME: 15 minutes
COOKING TIME: 2 hours on high or 6 hours on low
ADDITIONAL STEPS: Brown the sausage, if desired

INGREDIENTS

- **1¹/₂ pounds (685 g) peppers (about 3 average-size)**

- Cooking oil (optional)

- **1 pound (455 g) Italian sausage links**

- **1 cup (245 g) bottled marinara sauce**

Core the peppers and slice them into ¹/₂-inch (1-cm) strips. Put the peppers into the slow cooker. If desired, heat a large sauté pan over high heat and add 1 tablespoon (15 ml) or so of oil. Add the sausages and brown on all sides. Add the sausages to the slow cooker. You can skip the browning step if you want. Pour the marinara sauce over all and cook for 2 hours on high or 6 hours on low.

YIELD: *4 servings*

NUTRITIONAL ANALYSIS

466 calories; 37g fat (71.6% calories from fat); 18g protein; 15g carbohydrate; 4g dietary fiber; 86mg cholesterol; 1090mg sodium.

➕ ADD IT IN!

Slice up two medium-size onions and add them with the peppers.

 Mexican Pork Tinga

A tinga is a slow-cooked meat that is then pulled into shreds and typically heaped onto tostadas.

PREP TIME: 10 minutes

COOKING TIME: 10¹/₂ hours

ADDITIONAL STEPS: Allow the meat to cool enough to handle after cooking

INGREDIENTS

- **1 pork shoulder (about 5 pounds or 2275 g)**

- **1 (16-ounce or 455-g) jar roasted tomato salsa**

- **1 cup (235 ml) Malta Goya or similar malt drink, or beer**

Put the pork shoulder into the slow cooker and pour the salsa and malt drink over it. Cook on low for 10 hours. Remove the meat from the cooker, leaving the juices in the pot and the cooker on low. Allow the meat to cool, and then shred it with your hands or with tongs. Return the shredded meat to the slow cooker, stir into the sauce, and reheat for ¹/₂ hour.

 SERVING SUGGESTION: *Serve with tostadas and a variety of Mexican toppings.*

YIELD: *8 to 10 servings*

NUTRITIONAL ANALYSIS

424 calories; 31 g fat (67.3% calories from fat); 30g protein; 4g carbohydrate; 1g dietary fiber; 121mg cholesterol; 309mg sodium.

Orange-Glazed Ham

This is an easy way to bake a ham and leave the oven available for the rest of the dinner.

PREP TIME: 10 minutes
COOKING TIME: 3–4 hours on high or 7–8 hours on low

INGREDIENTS

- **1 semi-boneless ham (about 6 pounds or 2730 g)**
- **1 (12-ounce or 340-g) jar orange marmalade**
- **4 or 5 whole cloves**

Place the ham in the slow cooker. Slather the marmalade over the ham and stick the cloves into the ham. Cook on high for 3 to 4 hours or on low for 7 to 8 hours.

YIELD: *8 to 10 servings*

NUTRITIONAL ANALYSIS

590 calories; 29g fat (44.9% calories from fat); 48g protein; 33g carbohydrate; 1g dietary fiber; 155mg cholesterol; 3615mg sodium.

Plantain-Stuffed Pork Tenderloin Braised in Tomatillo Sauce

This dish involves a little more prep work than many in this book, but it is very much worth it. Serve with rice, black beans, and warm tortillas.

PREP TIME: 45 minutes
COOKING TIME: 2 hours on high or 4–5 hours on low
ADDITIONAL STEPS: Prepare the pork tenderloin rolls

INGREDIENTS

- **2 pork tenderloins (about 1 1/2 pounds or 685 g)**

- Salt and pepper to taste

- **1 medium-size ripe plantain**

- Cooking oil

- **1 (16-ounce or 455-g) jar tomatillo salsa (also called salsa verde)**

ADDITIONAL MATERIALS

- Butcher's twine

Trim any fat and silver skin (the thin, pearlescent membrane) from the tenderloins. Cut them in half across. Split each half lengthwise, leaving one side still attached. Lay out the meat pieces on a cutting board and lightly pound them to a uniform thickness. Season the meat with salt and pepper.

Peel the plantain and cut it into slices. Heat a sauté pan over medium-high heat and add a couple of tablespoons (30 ml) of oil. Sauté the plantain until lightly browned. Allow to cool.

Put some of the plantain in the center of each piece of pork and roll them up, tucking in the ends. Tie the rolls with butcher's twine. Reheat the sauté pan over medium-high heat and add a little more oil. Sear the tenderloin rolls in the sauté pan until browned on each side.

Put the pork rolls into the slow cooker and add the tomatillo sauce. Cook for 2 hours on high or 4 to 5 hours on low. Remove the pork from the cooker and remove the twine. Slice the rolls and put the slices on each of 4 plates. Spoon some of the sauce over the meat.

YIELD: *4 servings*

NUTRITIONAL ANALYSIS

299 calories; 6g fat (18.7% calories from fat); 36g protein; 22g carbohydrate; 1 g dietary fiber; 111 mg cholesterol; 459mg sodium.

✚ ADD IT IN!

Sprinkle some chopped fresh cilantro in with the salsa verde.

Pork and Black Bean Stew

Serve with tortillas, fresh cilantro, and lime wedges for an authentic Mexican treat.

PREP TIME: 20 minutes

COOKING TIME: 2–3 hours on high or 5–6 hours on low

INGREDIENTS

- **2 pounds (910 g) lean pork, such as loin**

- **2 (14-ounce or 395-g) cans black beans**

- **1 (16-ounce or 455-g) jar salsa**

- Salt and pepper to taste

Trim the fat from the pork. Cut the pork into 1-inch (2.5-cm) cubes and put them into the slow cooker. Drain the beans and add them to the pork. Add the salsa and stir. Cook for 2 to 3 hours on high or 5 to 6 hours on low. Adjust the seasoning with salt and pepper to taste.

YIELD: *6 to 8 servings*

NUTRITIONAL ANALYSIS

196 calories; 5g fat (22.6% calories from fat); 20g protein; 17g carbohydrate; 6g dietary fiber; 36mg cholesterol; 580mg sodium.

 Pork Chops Braised with Fennel

Fennel's licorice bite fades to a wonderful sweetness with slow cooking.

PREP TIME: 20 minutes
COOKING TIME: 5–6 hours
ADDITIONAL STEPS: Brown the pork chops before adding to the slow cooker

INGREDIENTS

- **4 (8-ounce or 225-g) center-cut pork chops, bone-in**

- Salt and pepper to taste

- Cooking oil

- **2 medium-size fennel bulbs**

- **$1/2$ cup (120 ml) apple juice**

Season the pork chops with salt and pepper. Heat a large sauté pan over medium-high heat and add a couple of tablespoons (30 ml) of oil. Add the pork chops and brown on both sides, about 5 minutes per side. Cut the top stalk off of the fennel bulbs and discard. Trim away any damaged outside layers from the fennel bulbs and trim the root ends. Cut each bulb into 6 to 8 wedges.

Put the fennel into the slow cooker and top with the pork chops. Pour the apple juice over. Cook for 5 to 6 hours on low. Serve each chop with some of the braised fennel and some of the pan juices spooned over the top.

YIELD: *4 servings*

NUTRITIONAL ANALYSIS

401 calories; 23g fat (51.1 % calories from fat); 36g protein; 12g carbohydrate; 4g dietary fiber; 112mg cholesterol; 150mg sodium.

Pork Roast with Orange and Ginger

This delicious citrus-infused roast is both elegant and easy. It makes a great meal for company when paired with rice pilaf and sautéed sugar snap peas.

PREP TIME: 30 minutes

COOKING TIME: 6–7 hours

ADDITIONAL STEPS: Brown the meat before adding to the slow cooker; degrease and reduce the cooking liquid

INGREDIENTS

- **1 pork loin roast, bone-in (about 5 pounds or 2275 g)**

- Salt and pepper to taste

- Cooking oil

- **2 tablespoons (12 g) minced fresh ginger root**

- **1 cup (235 ml) orange juice**

Season the pork loin with salt and pepper to taste. Heat a large sauté pan over medium-high heat. Add a couple of tablespoons (30 ml) of oil, add the pork loin, and sear, fatty side down, until nicely browned.

Put the pork loin into the slow cooker and spread the ginger on top. Pour in the orange juice. Cook for 6 to 7 hours on low. Remove the roast and keep it warm. Degrease the liquid in the slow cooker and reduce in a saucepan over high heat until slightly thickened. Serve the pork with the sauce.

YIELD: *4 to 6 servings*

NUTRITIONAL ANALYSIS

341 calories; 13g fat (35.8% calories from fat); 48g protein; 5g carbohydrate; trace dietary fiber; 119mg cholesterol; 98mg sodium.

✚ ADD IT IN!

Thicken the sauce by whisking together 1 tablespoon (8 g) cornstarch with 1/4 cup (60 ml) of the cooking liquid. Add to the rest of the sauce and whisk until thickened.

Roast Pork Loin with Honey Mustard

This recipe produces a juicy, tender, and delectable pork roast.

PREP TIME: 30 minutes

COOKING TIME: 6–7 hours

ADDITIONAL STEPS: Brown the meat before adding to the slow cooker

INGREDIENTS

- **1 pork loin roast, bone-in (about 5 pounds or 2275 g)**

- Salt and pepper to taste

- Cooking oil

- **3 medium-size onions**

- **1 cup (250 g) honey mustard**

Season the pork roast with salt and pepper. Heat a large sauté pan over medium-high heat and add a couple of tablespoons (30 ml) of oil. Add the roast. Sear the meat, fatty side down, until nicely browned.

Skin the onions and slice them into ¹/₂-inch-thick (1-cm) slices. Put the onions into the slow cooker. Put the pork roast on top of the onions and smear the honey mustard on the pork. Cook for 6 to 7 hours on low. Serve the pork with the braised onions from the pan, or use the onions and accumulated juices to make a gravy, if desired.

YIELD: *4 to 6 servings*

NUTRITIONAL ANALYSIS

380 calories; 16g fat (38.4% calories from fat); 51 g protein; 8g carbohydrate; 1g dietary fiber; 119mg cholesterol; 643mg sodium. Exchanges: 0 Grain(Starch); 7 Lean Meat; 1 Vegetable; ¹/₂ Fat.

Sausage Gravy

This is delicious served over fresh biscuits for a great Southern-style breakfast treat. Start the dish the night before, and the aroma will have you leaping out of bed in the morning.

PREP TIME: 10 minutes
COOKING TIME: 8 hours
ADDITIONAL STEPS: Add flour and milk after 1 hour

INGREDIENTS

- **1 pound (455 g) bulk breakfast sausage**

- **¹/₂ cup (60 g) all-purpose flour**

- **2 cups (470 ml) milk**

- Salt and pepper to taste

Break up the sausage into small bits and put into the slow cooker. Cook on high for 1 hour. Stir well to break the sausage into small "pebbles." Stir in the flour until absorbed. Stir in the milk. Add salt and pepper to taste. Turn the cooker to low and cook for 6 to 7 hours.

 SERVING SUGGESTION: *Make some quick biscuits to serve as a base for the sausage gravy.*

YIELD: *4 to 6 servings*

NUTRITIONAL ANALYSIS

403 calories; 33g fat (74.9% calories from fat); 13g protein; 12g carbohydrate; trace dietary fiber; 63mg cholesterol; 545mg sodium.

Smoked Ham Hocks with White Beans

If you're going to cook beans in a slow cooker, you must presoak them. You can do this by soaking the beans in cool water overnight, then draining them and adding them to the recipe. A faster method is to cover the beans with plenty of water in a saucepan, bring them to a boil, remove them from the heat, keep them covered, and allow them to stand for 1 hour. Drain the beans and proceed with the recipe.

PREP TIME: 10 minutes
COOKING TIME: 8–10 hours

INGREDIENTS

- **1 pound (455 g) great Northern or other white beans, presoaked**

- **2 pounds (910 g) smoked ham hocks**

- **4 cups (940 ml) chicken stock or broth**

- Pepper to taste

Put the beans and the ham hocks into the slow cooker. Add the chicken stock and enough water so you have about twice as much liquid as beans. Cook on low for 8 to 10 hours, until the beans are tender and the liquid is absorbed. Check and add liquid during the cooking as needed to keep the beans from going dry.

YIELD: *4 servings*

NUTRITIONAL ANALYSIS

1006 calories; 44g fat (40.3% calories from fat); 76g protein; 72g carbohydrate; 23g dietary fiber; 241 mg cholesterol; 2304mg sodium.

✚ ADD IT IN!

Stir in 1 or 2 tablespoons (2.5 to 5 g) chopped fresh thyme to add another flavor dimension.

Stuffed Pork Chops

The rice and vegetable stuffing practically makes these chops a meal in themselves.

PREP TIME: 30 minutes
COOKING TIME: 4–5 hours
ADDITIONAL STEPS: Brown the pork chops before adding to the slow cooker

INGREDIENTS

- **4 (1-inch- or 2.5-cm-thick) pork chops (about 2 pounds or 910 g)**

- **1 (8-ounce or 225-g) package cooked rice with vegetables**

- Salt and pepper to taste

- Cooking oil

- **1 cup (235 ml) chicken stock or broth**

Cut a pocket in the side of each chop, and stuff each one with some of the rice mixture. Close the pocket by securing with a toothpick. Heat a large sauté pan over medium-high heat. Season the chops with salt and pepper and add a couple of tablespoons (30 ml) of oil to the hot pan. Add the chops and brown on each side, about 5 minutes per side, working in batches, if necessary, to avoid crowding the pan.

Put the chops into the slow cooker and add the stock. Cook on low for 4 to 4 1/2 hours. You can degrease the pan juices and reduce them for a sauce, if desired.

YIELD: *4 servings*

NUTRITIONAL ANALYSIS

403 calories; 22g fat (52.1 % calories from fat); 36g protein; 10g carbohydrate; 1 g dietary fiber; 112mg cholesterol; 689mg sodium.

🐖 Thai Curry Pork

This luscious dish is perfect served with steamed jasmine rice. (You'll want to spoon the sauce over the rice as well as the ribs.) Feel free to add more curry paste if you want a spicier dish.

PREP TIME: 10 minutes
COOKING TIME: 8 hours
ADDITIONAL STEPS: Add more coconut milk in the last ¹/₂ hour

INGREDIENTS

- **2 pounds (910 g) country-style pork ribs**

- **2 tablespoons (32 g) Thai red curry paste**

- **1 cup (235 ml) coconut milk, divided**

Place the country-style ribs in the slow cooker and rub the curry paste on the meat. Add ¹/₂ cup (120 ml) of the coconut milk and cook on low for 7 to 8 hours. Add the remaining ¹/₂ cup (120 ml) coconut milk in the final ¹/₂ hour of cooking.

YIELD: *4 servings*

NUTRITIONAL ANALYSIS

583 calories; 51 g fat (79.3% calories from fat); 26g protein; 4g carbohydrate; 2g dietary fiber; 111 mg cholesterol; 339mg sodium.

Honey Dijon Pork Cutlets

There is nothing better than coming home after work to a meal that's two-thirds of the way prepared. Here, just add some biscuits or rice and you are good to go.

PREP TIME: 10 minutes
COOKING TIME: 3 hours on high or 6 hours on low
ADDITIONAL STEPS: Add the vegetables 1 hour before the dish is done

INGREDIENTS

- 2¹/₂ pounds (1140 g) pork sirloin cutlets

- 1 cup (235 ml) honey Dijon marinade

- 1 (14-ounce or 395-g) bag frozen baby potato vegetable blend, thawed

Put the pork cutlets into the slow cooker and pour the honey Dijon marinade over them. Cook on high for 2 hours or on low for 5 hours. Add the thawed vegetables and cook for 1 hour longer.

YIELD: *4 to 6 servings*

NUTRITIONAL ANALYSIS

440 calories; 22g fat (48.7% calories from fat); 28g protein; 26g carbohydrate; 2g dietary fiber; 90mg cholesterol; 159mg sodium.

 Pork Chops Braised with Sauerkraut

You'll swear you're in Alsace! Serve with mashed potatoes and warm home-made applesauce for a cozy dinner.

PREP TIME: 30 minutes

COOKING TIME: 5–6 hours

ADDITIONAL STEPS: Brown the chops before adding to the slow cooker

INGREDIENTS

- **4 center-cut pork chops (about 2 pounds or 910 g)**

- Salt and pepper to taste

- Cooking oil

- **1 (16-ounce or 455-g) package sauerkraut**

- **1 cup (235 ml) white wine**

Season the chops with salt and pepper to taste. Heat a large sauté pan over medium-high heat. Add a couple of tablespoons (30 ml) of oil, then add the chops, turning them after a few minutes to brown both sides.

Put the chops into the slow cooker. Rinse the sauerkraut for a minute under cold water in a colander and allow to drain. Add the rinsed sauerkraut to the slow cooker. Add the wine. Cook for 5 to 6 hours on low.

YIELD: *4 servings*

NUTRITIONAL ANALYSIS

412 calories; 22g fat (55.0% calories from fat); 36g protein; 5g carbohydrate; 3g dietary fiber; 112mg cholesterol; 841 mg sodium.

🐖 Sausage with Apples and Onions

This dish is so adaptable it can be served on nearly any occasion. Serve it with pancakes for a hearty breakfast, or pair it with mashed potatoes for a delicious dinner.

PREP TIME: 30 minutes
COOKING TIME: 2–3 hours on high or 6–8 hours on low
ADDITIONAL STEPS: Sauté the apples, onions, and sausages

INGREDIENTS

- **2 pounds (910 g) apples**

- **4 medium-size onions**

- Cooking oil

- Salt and pepper to taste

- **1 pound (455 g) breakfast sausage links**

Peel and core the apples and cut them into ¼-inch-thick (6-mm-thick) slices. Peel the onions and julienne them ¼ inch (6 mm) thick. Heat a large sauté pan over medium-high heat. Add enough oil to coat the pan and add the apples and onions. Season with salt and pepper to taste. Sauté, tossing occasionally, until lightly browned. Put the sautéed apples and onions into the slow cooker. Add the sausage links to the sauté pan and brown on all sides for a few minutes. Add them to the slow cooker. Cook on high for 2 to 3 hours or on low for 6 to 8 hours.

YIELD: *4 to 6 servings*

NUTRITIONAL ANALYSIS

426 calories; 31 g fat (64.6% calories from fat); 10g protein; 28g carbohydrate; 5g dietary fiber; 51 mg cholesterol; 507mg sodium.

 Smoked Shoulder Braised in Cider

Pork and apples are classic flavor buddies. In this recipe, cider, cloves, and pepper add a deeper, more complex taste to the beloved combination.

PREP TIME: 10 minutes
COOKING TIME: 8–10 hours

INGREDIENTS

- **1 smoked pork shoulder (about 5 pounds or 2275 g)**

- **2 cups (470 ml) apple cider**

- **4 whole cloves**

- Pepper to taste

Put the pork shoulder into the slow cooker. Add the cider, cloves, and pepper to taste. Cook on low for 8 to 10 hours. Remove the pork shoulder from the cooker and slice.

YIELD: *6 to 8 servings*

NUTRITIONAL ANALYSIS

542 calories; 39g fat (65.6% calories from fat); 37g protein; 9g carbohydrate; 1g dietary fiber; 151mg cholesterol; 148mg sodium.

✚ ADD IT IN!

Core, peel, and slice 3 or 4 apples and add them to the cooker for some applesauce.

🐖 Easy Maple Barbecue Pulled Pork

Pulled pork is a classic Southern barbecue treat. Here, we add a Northern twist with maple syrup.

PREP TIME: 10 minutes

COOKING TIME: 8 1/2–9 hours

ADDITIONAL STEPS: Cool and shred the pork

INGREDIENTS

- **1 pork shoulder roast (about 5 pounds or 2275 g)**

- **2 cups (500 g) barbecue sauce, divided**

- **1/2 cup (170 g) maple syrup**

Put the pork, 1 cup (250 g) of the barbecue sauce, and the maple syrup into the slow cooker. Cook for 8 hours on low. Remove the pork from the cooker and allow to cool enough to handle. Shred the meat, discarding the bones. Degrease the liquid from the slow cooker. Add the shredded meat and the liquid back into the slow cooker along with the remaining 1 cup (250 g) barbecue sauce. Cook for another 1/2 to 1 hour.

 SERVING SUGGESTION: *Serve with some red beans and rice, or on a bun as a sandwich.*

YIELD: *8 to 10 servings*

NUTRITIONAL ANALYSIS

481 calories; 32g fat (60.1% calories from fat); 30g protein; 17g carbohydrate; 1g dietary fiber; 121mg cholesterol; 520mg sodium.

CHAPTER 7
FISH AND SEAFOOD

Slow cookers aren't traditionally linked with fish cookery. That's chiefly because so many dishes are designed to be in the pot all day, and such a long cooking time will either make fish tough or dissolve it into a paste. But that's not to say that a slow cooker can't be used for fish—it's all in the way you approach it. This slow, moist heat is perfect for poaching, and some of the firmer fish take well to braising, too. Although you can't "set and forget" fish recipes to the same extent as other dishes, Garlic Clams (page 144) or Mussels with Wine and Pesto (page 149) would make a perfect appetizer next time you have friends over for a backyard gathering. Quick, easy, and completely free of last-minute preparation—sounds like a recipe for dinner-party success to us!

# Calamari Fra Diavolo

Fra diavolo, which means "brother devil," is a traditional spicy red sauce, and here it gives a lovely kick to calamari. Calamari must either be cooked very fast at high heat or very slowly at low heat to be tender. We are using a slow cooker, so of course we opt for the latter. Ratchet up the pepper heat to your own taste.

PREP TIME: 15 minutes
COOKING TIME: 2 hours

INGREDIENTS

- **2 pounds (910 g) calamari rings and tentacles**

- **2 cups (490 g) marinara sauce**

- **2 tablespoons (7 g) red pepper flakes**

- Salt and pepper to taste

Put the calamari into the slow cooker. Add the marinara sauce and red pepper flakes, along with salt and pepper to taste. Cook on low for 2 hours.

 SERVING SUGGESTION: *This is terrific served over linguine.*

YIELD: *4 servings*

NUTRITIONAL ANALYSIS

281 calories; 6g fat (19.0% calories from fat); 37g protein; 17g carbohydrate; 2g dietary fiber; 529mg cholesterol; 615mg sodium.

 # Catfish and Beans

Here's a slow-cooker twist on a classic Southern taste combo.

PREP TIME: 10 minutes
COOKING TIME: 1 hour on high or 2 hours on low

INGREDIENTS

- **2 pounds (910 g) catfish fillets**

- Salt and pepper to taste

- **1 (14-ounce or 395-g) can pinto beans, drained and rinsed**

- **1 (12-ounce or 340-g) can diced tomatoes with onions and peppers**

Put the catfish into the slow cooker and season with salt and pepper. Pour the beans over the fish and add the tomatoes. Cook for 1 hour on high or 2 hours on low, until the fish is firm and cooked through. Serve the catfish with some of the beans and sauce.

 SERVING SUGGESTION: *This dish tastes great with hush puppies.*

YIELD: *4 servings*

NUTRITIONAL ANALYSIS

311 calories; 7g fat (20.5% calories from fat); 42g protein; 18g carbohydrate; 4g dietary fiber; 132mg cholesterol; 518mg sodium.

 Cod and Broccoli Casserole

Any white fish, such as haddock, pollock, or sole, will work well in this yummy casserole.

PREP TIME: 15 minutes

COOKING TIME: 1 hour on high or 2 hours on low

ADDITIONAL STEPS: Add the fish and cracker crumbs after $1/2$ hour

INGREDIENTS

- **1 (16-ounce or 455-g) package frozen broccoli in cheese sauce**

- **1-pound (455-g) cod fillet**

- Salt and pepper to taste

- **1 cup (100 g) buttery cracker crumbs, such as Ritz**

Put the broccoli and cheese sauce into the slow cooker and cook on high for $1/2$ hour or on low for 1 hour. Lay the cod on top of the broccoli and season with salt and pepper. Sprinkle the cracker crumbs over the fish, and continue cooking for $1/2$ hour on high or 1 hour on low, until the fish is firm, opaque, and flakes when cut.

YIELD: *4 servings*

NUTRITIONAL ANALYSIS

278 calories; 7g fat (21.7% calories from fat); 25g protein; 28g carbohydrate; 1g dietary fiber; 49mg cholesterol; 931 mg sodium.

 Crab Hot Pot

You can use Dungeness crab, snow crab claws, king crab, or, of course, blue crab for this dish.

PREP TIME: 10 minutes
COOKING TIME: 1–2 hours

INGREDIENTS

- **4 pounds (1820 g) whole crabs or cut-up pieces of king crabs**

- **¼ cup (25 g) crab boil, such as Old Bay**

- **1 cup (235 ml) white wine**

Put the crabs into the slow cooker. Sprinkle the seasoning over them and add the wine. Cook for 1 to 2 hours on high, until the crabs are red. Serve with melted butter for dipping.

YIELD: *4 servings*

NUTRITIONAL ANALYSIS

421 calories; 3g fat (6.8% calories from fat); 83g protein; trace carbohydrate; 0g dietary fiber; 191mg cholesterol; 3996mg sodium.

Creamed Lobster

Creamed lobster is something that our grandmother would have ordered for lunch at the yacht club, where she regularly terrorized the daytime waitstaff. While this may be a bit old school, it does make for an elegant and sinfully rich meal.

PREP TIME: 10 minutes
COOKING TIME: 1 hour

INGREDIENTS

- **1 pound (455 g) cooked lobster meat**

- **1 (12-ounce or 355-ml) can condensed cream of celery soup**

- **1 cup (115 g) shredded Monterey Jack cheese**

Put the lobster meat into the slow cooker. Add the soup and sprinkle the cheese over the top. Cook for $1/2$ hour on low, then stir and cook for another $1/2$ hour, until the cheese is melted and the lobster is heated through.

SERVING SUGGESTION: *Serve over rice or toast points, or in pastry shells (you can find them in the freezer section of the grocery store; prepare them according to the package directions).*

YIELD: *4 servings*

NUTRITIONAL ANALYSIS

248 calories; 11 g fat (41.5% calories from fat); 31 g protein; 5g carbohydrate; trace dietary fiber; 112mg cholesterol; 914mg sodium.

 # Garlic Clams

Use fresh garlic if at all possible, rather than the bottled minced product. This makes an absolutely fabulous, although messy, snack-type food for a casual get-together.

PREP TIME: 10 minutes
COOKING TIME: 1 hour

INGREDIENTS

- **1 cup (235 ml) white wine**

- **2 pounds (910 g) littleneck clams**

- **¼ cup (38 g) minced garlic**

- Salt and pepper to taste

Put the wine into the slow cooker and turn it on high. Rinse the clams and discard any that are open and do not close when tapped. Add the clams to the slow cooker. Add the garlic and salt and pepper to taste. Cook for about 1 hour, until the clams are open and tender. Serve in bowls with some of the cooking juices.

 SERVING SUGGESTION: *Get a loaf of crusty French bread and tear off chunks to sop up the broth. Good stuff!*

YIELD: *4 servings*

NUTRITIONAL ANALYSIS

221 calories; 2g fat (11.5% calories from fat); 30g protein; 9g carbohydrate; trace dietary fiber; 77mg cholesterol; 131mg sodium.

Lemon Pepper Clams

These clams have a zesty citrus tang to them that is sure to delight.

PREP TIME: 10 minutes

COOKING TIME: 1 hour

INGREDIENTS

- **1 cup (235 ml) white wine**

- **2 pounds (910 g) littleneck clams**

- **¹/₂ cup (120 ml) lemon pepper marinade**

Put the wine into the slow cooker and turn it on high. Rinse the clams and discard any that are open and do not close when tapped. Add the clams to the slow cooker. Add the lemon pepper marinade. Cook for about 1 hour on high, until the clams are open and tender. Serve in bowls with some of the cooking juices.

YIELD: *4 servings*

NUTRITIONAL ANALYSIS

244 calories; 3g fat (12.3% calories from fat); 30g protein; 13g carbohydrate; 1g dietary fiber; 77mg cholesterol; 2170mg sodium.

 Manhattan Braised Halibut

The firm texture of halibut makes it a natural for braising in the slow cooker.

PREP TIME: 10 minutes

COOKING TIME: 2 hours

INGREDIENTS

- **4 halibut steaks (about 2 pounds or 910 g)**

- **1 (14-ounce or 355-ml) can Manhattan-style clam chowder**

- **1 tablespoon (8 g) cornstarch**

Put the halibut into the slow cooker and pour the clam chowder over it. Cook on low for 1½ hours, until the halibut is firm and cooked through. Remove the halibut from the cooker and keep warm. Turn the cooker up to high. Mix the cornstarch with enough water to make a slurry, then stir it into the pan juices. Stir until the sauce clears and thickens a little. Put the halibut on plates and pour some of the sauce over it.

YIELD: *4 servings*

NUTRITIONAL ANALYSIS

289 calories; 6g fat (20.0% calories from fat); 48g protein; 7g carbohydrate; 1g dietary fiber; 74mg cholesterol; 358mg sodium.

Mexican Braised Mahi Mahi

The firm texture and succulence of mahi mahi is perfect for this braised dish. You can also substitute wahoo or swordfish.

PREP TIME: 10 minutes
COOKING TIME: 1 hour on high or 2 hours on low
ADDITIONAL STEPS: Add the pineapple in the last few minutes of cooking

INGREDIENTS

- **4 pieces mahi mahi (about 1½ pounds or 685 g)**

- Salt and pepper to taste

- **1 (14-ounce or 395-g) can diced Mexican tomatoes with chiles and cilantro**

- **1 (8-ounce or 225-g) can pineapple chunks**

Put the mahi mahi into the slow cooker and season with salt and pepper. Add the diced tomatoes and cook for 45 to 50 minutes on high or 1 hour 45 minutes on low, until the fish is cooked through. Drain the pineapple and add it to the slow cooker. Cook for another 10 to 15 minutes. Serve the fish with some of the sauce and pineapple over it.

YIELD: *4 servings*

NUTRITIONAL ANALYSIS

55 calories; trace fat (5.4% calories from fat); 1g protein; 14g carbohydrate; 1g dietary fiber; 0mg cholesterol; 9mg sodium.

✚ ADD IT IN!

Sprinkle fresh chopped cilantro and squeeze a wedge of lime over each serving. You can also add more chopped chiles to the pot if you want a spicier dish.

Mussels with Marinara

This is a classic dish for good reason—it's delicious!

PREP TIME: 10 minutes

COOKING TIME: 1 hour

INGREDIENTS

- **1 cup (235 ml) white wine**

- **2 pounds (910 g) mussels**

- **1 cup (245 g) marinara sauce**

Put the wine into the slow cooker and turn it on high. Rinse the mussels and discard any that are open and do not close when tapped. Add the mussels to the slow cooker. Add the marinara sauce. Cook for about 1 hour on high, until the mussels are open and tender. Serve in bowls with some of the sauce.

YIELD: *4 servings*

NUTRITIONAL ANALYSIS

271 calories; 6g fat (25.2% calories from fat); 28g protein; 14g carbohydrate; 1g dietary fiber; 64mg cholesterol; 91 0mg sodium.

➕ ADD IT IN!

The Brotherhood of Garlic-Lovin' Fools would like to point out that a couple of cloves of chopped garlic would spice this up nicely.

Mussels with Wine and Pesto

Tender mussels steamed in wine fragrant with basil and garlic. Oh yeah!

PREP TIME: 10 minutes
COOKING TIME: 1 hour

INGREDIENTS

- **1 cup (235 ml) white wine**

- **2 pounds (910 g) mussels**

- **½ cup (130 g) basil pesto**

Put the wine into the slow cooker and turn it on high. Rinse the mussels and discard any that are open and do not close when tapped. Add the mussels to the slow cooker. Add the pesto. Cook for about 1 hour on high, until the mussels are open and tender. Serve in bowls with some of the cooking juices.

YIELD: *4 servings*

NUTRITIONAL ANALYSIS

387 calories; 19g fat (50.0% calories from fat); 32g protein; 11 g carbohydrate; trace dietary fiber; 72mg cholesterol; 858mg sodium.

✚ ADD IT IN!

More Garlic! More Garlic!

Olive-Oil-Poached Tuna

This one may not fall under the category of comfort food classics, but it sure is good! The oil infuses the flavors of the pesto into the fish, and the texture is like butter.

PREP TIME: 10 minutes

COOKING TIME: 1 hour

ADDITIONAL STEPS: Add the pesto and tuna for the last 10–15 minutes

INGREDIENTS

- **3 cups (705 ml) extra-virgin olive oil**

- **¹/₂ cup (130 g) basil pesto**

- **4 tuna steaks (about 2 pounds or 910 g)**

- Salt and pepper to taste

Put the olive oil into the slow cooker and heat on low for about 40 minutes. Stir in the pesto and heat for another 5 minutes. Season the tuna with salt and pepper and add to the slow cooker. Cook for 10 to 12 minutes for medium fish, less for rare, more for well done. Carefully remove the tuna from the slow cooker using a slotted spoon.

YIELD: *4 servings*

NUTRITIONAL ANALYSIS

1911 calories; 187g fat (87.5% calories from fat); 58g protein; 2g carbohydrate; trace dietary fiber; 95mg cholesterol; 295mg sodium.

Poached Salmon in Creamy Lemon Sauce

Delicate salmon with a piquant sauce. This is a classy and classic dish that's great for your next dinner party.

PREP TIME: 10 minutes
COOKING TIME: 1 hour
ADDITIONAL STEPS: Stir in the crème fraîche just before serving

INGREDIENTS

- **4 pieces salmon fillet (about 1¹/₂ pounds or 685 g)**

- Salt and pepper to taste

- **2 tablespoons (30 ml) lemon juice**

- **¹/₂ cup (115 g) crème fraîche**

Put the salmon into the slow cooker and season with salt and pepper. Pour the lemon juice over the fish and cook for 1 hour on low. Carefully remove the fish from the slow cooker and whisk the crème fraîche into the pan juices. Pour some of the sauce over each piece of fish.

YIELD: *4 servings*

NUTRITIONAL ANALYSIS

282 calories; 14g fat (47.1 % calories from fat); 35g protein; 2g carbohydrate; trace dietary fiber; 115mg cholesterol; 127mg sodium.

✚ ADD IT IN!

Sprinkle fresh chopped chives or chervil over each serving.

Salt Cod with Onions and Tomatoes

Salt cod is the ultimate comfort food for many of Italian and Portuguese ancestry. One must never overcook salt cod, or it will be tough. The slow cooker is great for the gentle cooking required.

PREP TIME: 20 minutes

COOKING TIME: 2 hours on high or 3–4 hours on low

ADDITIONAL STEPS: Refresh the cod before cooking; add the cod to the slow cooker for the last ¹/₂ or 1 hour of the cooking time

INGREDIENTS

- **1 pound (455 g) salt cod, refreshed**

- **2 pounds (910 g) onions**

- **1 (14-ounce or 395-g) can diced tomatoes with herbs and garlic**

To refresh the salt cod, soak the cod in cold water for 3 days in the refrigerator, changing the water daily.

Peel the onions and slice them thin. Put the onions into the slow cooker and add the tomatoes. Cook for 1¹/₂ hours on high or 3 hours on low. Add the cod, nestling it into the onions and sauce. Continue cooking for ¹/₂ hour on high or 1 hour on low, until the cod is tender and flakes. Serve the cod with some of the sauce and onions.

 SERVING SUGGESTION: *Simple boiled potatoes are a great accompaniment.*

YIELD: *4 servings*

NUTRITIONAL ANALYSIS

428 calories; 3g fat (7.2% calories from fat); 74g protein; 22g carbohydrate; 5g dietary fiber; 173mg cholesterol; 7991 mg sodium.

Scallops with Spinach and Cheese Sauce

Quick and easy and oh, so good. Buy fresh-pack (also known as natural) scallops.

PREP TIME: 20 minutes

COOKING TIME: 1 hour

ADDITIONAL STEPS: Precook the spinach

INGREDIENTS

- **1 pound (455 g) fresh spinach**

- **1 pound (455 g) sea scallops, side muscles removed**

- **1 (12-ounce or 355-ml) can cheddar cheese soup**

Put the spinach into a large pot with 2 cups (470 ml) water. Cook over high heat only until the spinach wilts. Remove and drain well.

Put the scallops into the slow cooker, then top with the cooked spinach. Pour the cheddar soup over all. Cook for 1 hour on high.

YIELD: *4 servings*

NUTRITIONAL ANALYSIS

178 calories; 5g fat (23.9% calories from fat); 24g protein; 10g carbohydrate; 3g dietary fiber; 48mg cholesterol; 602mg sodium.

Simple Shrimp Jambalaya

This is a vastly simplified version of a very complex dish, but it's still quite tasty.

PREP TIME: 10 minutes
COOKING TIME: 1¹/₂ hours on high or 3 hours on low
ADDITIONAL STEPS: Add the shrimp toward the end of cooking

INGREDIENTS

- **2 cups (390 g) uncooked white rice**

- **1 (14-ounce 395-g) can diced tomatoes with peppers and onions**

- Salt and pepper to taste

- **1 pound (455 g) shelled shrimp**

Put the rice into the slow cooker. Add the tomatoes, salt and pepper to taste, and 3 cups (705 ml) water. Stir. Cook for 1 hour on high or 2 hours on low, until the rice is tender and most of the water is absorbed. Stir in the shrimp and continue to cook for another ¹/₂ hour on high or 1 hour on low, until all the water is absorbed and the shrimp are tender and pink.

YIELD: *4 servings*

NUTRITIONAL ANALYSIS

479 calories; 3g fat (5.5% calories from fat); 30g protein; 79g carbohydrate; 2g dietary fiber; 173mg cholesterol; 182mg sodium.

> **✚ ADD IT IN!**
>
> Slice up 1 pound (455 g) chorizo sausage and add it with the rice.

 # Spicy Shrimp with Peppers

Use a spicy marinara sauce, usually called fra diavolo (see page 139), to give this recipe its kick.

PREP TIME: 20 minutes
COOKING TIME: 1¹/₂ hours on high or 3 hours on low

INGREDIENTS

- **2 pounds (910 g) sweet bell peppers (about 3 or 4), whichever color you prefer**

- **3 cups (735 g) fra diavolo or other spicy marinara sauce**

- **2 pounds (910 g) shelled shrimp (20 to 24 count per pound or larger)**

Remove the tops from the peppers, cut out the seeds, and core. Cut the peppers into ¹/₂-inch (1-cm) rings and add to the slow cooker. Add the sauce and cook for 1 hour on high or 2 hours on low. Add the shrimp and continue to cook for ¹/₂ hour on high or 1 hour on low, until the shrimp are pink.

 SERVING SUGGESTION: *Serve over pasta or rice.*

YIELD: *4 to 6 servings*

NUTRITIONAL ANALYSIS

265 calories; 5g fat (18.5% calories from fat); 33g protein; 20g carbohydrate; 4g dietary fiber; 230mg cholesterol; 741 mg sodium.

◄ Sweet and Sour Shrimp

This easy and tasty Chinese meal is healthy and low in fat, too.

PREP TIME: 10 minutes

COOKING TIME: 1 hour on high or 2 hours on low

ADDITIONAL STEPS: Cook the vegetables and add them at the last minute

INGREDIENTS

- **2 pounds (910 g) shelled shrimp**

- **2 cups (450 g) Chinese sweet and sour sauce**

- **1 (1-pound or 455-g) bag frozen Chinese stir-fry vegetable mix**

Put the shrimp and sweet and sour sauce into the slow cooker. Cook for 1 hour on high or 2 hours on low, until the shrimp are pink, opaque, and firm.

When the shrimp are almost finished, put the vegetables into a saucepan with 1 cup (235 ml) water. Bring to a boil over high heat and cook for 2 to 3 minutes. Drain the vegetables well and add them to the slow cooker, stirring them into the shrimp and sauce.

 SERVING SUGGESTION: *Serve over white rice.*

YIELD: *4 to 6 servings*

NUTRITIONAL ANALYSIS

285 calories; 3g fat (8.3% calories from fat); 33g protein; 31 g carbohydrate; 2g dietary fiber; 230mg cholesterol; 497mg sodium.

Swordfish Braised with Thai Green Curry

Swordfish is a firm fish that's flavorful enough to take the warmth of a curry.

PREP TIME: 10 minutes
COOKING TIME: 2 hours

INGREDIENTS

- **4 swordfish steaks (about 2 pounds or 910 g)**

- **1 tablespoon (15 g) Thai green curry paste**

- **1 (12-ounce or 355-ml) can coconut milk**

Put the swordfish into the slow cooker. In a small bowl, mix together the green curry paste and the coconut milk. Pour over the swordfish and cook for about 2 hours on low, until the fish is cooked through but still tender. Serve the fish with some of the sauce.

YIELD: *4 servings*

NUTRITIONAL ANALYSIS

491 calories; 31 g fat (57.4% calories from fat); 47g protein; 5g carbohydrate; 2g dietary fiber; 89mg cholesterol; 329mg sodium.

Swordfish with Ginger and Soy

The clean taste of ginger makes a terrific foil for soy—great flavor buddies, as you'll see in this delicious dish.

PREP TIME: 10 minutes
COOKING TIME: 1 hour on high or 2 hours on low

INGREDIENTS

- **4 swordfish steaks (about 2 pounds or 910 g)**

- Salt and pepper to taste

- **2 tablespoons (12 g) peeled, minced fresh ginger root**

- **¼ cup (60 ml) soy sauce**

Put the swordfish into the slow cooker. Season with salt and pepper. Sprinkle with the ginger and pour the soy sauce over all. Cook for about 1 hour on high or 2 hours on low, until the fish is cooked through but still tender. Serve the fish with some of the sauce.

YIELD: *4 servings*

NUTRITIONAL ANALYSIS

286 calories; 9g fat (30.0% calories from fat); 46g protein; 2g carbohydrate; trace dietary fiber; 89mg cholesterol; 1233mg sodium.

CHAPTER 8
VEGETABLES

For most American families, vegetables have traditionally been relegated to the third and fourth slot in the meal, behind the meat and the starch. Although we certainly have improved from the old "boil it till it drops" philosophy of vegetable cookery, we could still do some work toward pulling veggies into the spotlight. Slow cookers offer a great way to do that, giving cooks a chance to use something besides a pot of water and a stove burner for their vegetable cookery. These recipes include more traditional side dishes that we've brightened with fresh flavor twists, such as Beets with Ginger and Orange (page 160), and others that could even double as vegetarian entrees, like Eggplant, Zucchini, and Tomato Layered Casserole (page 170). Expand your vegetable vocabulary with some of these dishes—your taste buds will thank you!

 Beets with Ginger and Orange

The sweet earthiness of beets is one of our favorites, and here it sparkles with the infusion of ginger and orange.

PREP TIME: 30 minutes
COOKING TIME: 3 hours on high or 6–7 hours on low

INGREDIENTS

- **3 pounds (1365 g) beets**

- Salt and pepper to taste

- **1 tablespoon (6 g) minced fresh ginger**

- **1 cup (235 ml) orange juice**

- 2 to 3 tablespoons (28 to 42 g) unsalted butter

Wash and peel the beets and slice them $\frac{1}{2}$ inch (1 cm) thick. Put the beets into the slow cooker and season with salt and pepper to taste. Sprinkle the ginger over the beets and pour the orange juice on top. Top with the butter cut into small pieces. Cook for 3 hours on high or 6 to 7 hours on low, until the beets are tender.

YIELD: *6 to 8 servings*

NUTRITIONAL ANALYSIS

102 calories; 5g fat (38.6% calories from fat); 2g protein; 14g carbohydrate; 3g dietary fiber; 12mg cholesterol; 133mg sodium.

 Braised Artichoke Hearts

We would happily eat these as a main dish, not a side, but then again we are helpless in the grip of our deep and abiding love for all things artichoke. (Kind of strange when you realize it's a member of the thistle family.)

PREP TIME: 10 minutes

COOKING TIME: 2 hours on high or 4–5 hours on low

INGREDIENTS

- **2 (12-ounce or 340-g) packages frozen artichoke hearts**

- **1 cup (180 g) canned diced tomatoes**

- **¹/₂ cup (120 ml) light cream**

- Salt and pepper to taste

Put the artichoke hearts into the slow cooker. Add the tomatoes and the cream and stir gently. Season with salt and pepper to taste. Cook for 2 hours on high or 4 to 5 hours on low. Stir and serve.

YIELD: *4 to 6 servings*

NUTRITIONAL ANALYSIS

99 calories; 5g fat (41.0% calories from fat); 3g protein; 12g carbohydrate; 7g dietary fiber; 13mg cholesterol; 85mg sodium.

> ✚ ADD IT IN!
>
> Sprinkle ¹/₂ cup (50 g) grated Parmesan cheese into the mixture.

 Braised Leeks with Vinaigrette

Hailing originally from the Mediterranean region, leeks have been prized for centuries—sometimes for the belief that they gave strength (sixth-century Wales) and sometimes just because their subtle, mild flavor is delicious (rest of the world). This dish can be served hot or cold, and is sure to delight either way. As always, make sure you thoroughly wash these buggers, as they hide bits of dirt with great enthusiasm.

PREP TIME: 20 minutes
COOKING TIME: 2 hours on high or 5–6 hours on low

INGREDIENTS

- **1 bunch leeks (usually 3 per bunch)**

- Salt and pepper to taste

- **¹/₂ cup (120 ml) Italian vinaigrette**

- **¹/₄ cup (30 g) chopped flat-leaf parsley**

Trim the root ends of the leeks and cut off the tough upper dark green parts. You can shave away some of the dark green to get to the tender light green part underneath. Split the leeks in half, lengthwise, and soak in lots of cold water for several minutes. It is important to soak leeks well to get out the grit between the layers of the vegetable.

Put the leeks into the slow cooker and add ¹/₂ cup (120 ml) water, along with salt and pepper to taste. Cook for 2 hours on high or 5 to 6 hours on low, until the leeks are very tender. Remove the leeks carefully from the cooker and put them on a serving plate to serve hot, or refrigerate if serving cold. Either way, when ready to serve, drizzle the leeks with the vinaigrette and top with the parsley.

YIELD: *4 servings*

NUTRITIONAL ANALYSIS

182 calories; 16g fat (75.5% calories from fat); 1g protein; 10g carbohydrate; 1g dietary fiber; 0mg cholesterol; 16mg sodium.

 Braised Red Cabbage

This savory dish is great with sausages, pot roast, and roast pork.

PREP TIME: 20 minutes

COOKING TIME: 3 hours on high or 6–7 hours on low

INGREDIENTS

- **1 head red cabbage (about 2 pounds or 910 g)**

- **½ cup (120 ml) red wine vinegar**

- **2 tablespoons (13 g) caraway seeds**

- Salt and pepper to taste

Core the cabbage and shred it. Add the cabbage to the slow cooker. Pour the vinegar over the cabbage and sprinkle with the caraway seeds. Season with salt and pepper to taste. Cook for 3 hours on high or 6 to 7 hours on low, until the cabbage is soft. Stir and serve.

YIELD: *6 to 8 servings*

NUTRITIONAL ANALYSIS

38 calories; 1g fat (10.3% calories from fat); 2g protein; 9g carbohydrate; 3g dietary fiber; 0mg cholesterol; 13mg sodium.

 Butternut Squash Puree

It doesn't get any easier than this slow-cooker method to make this fall classic. To make this dish even easier, buy the squash already peeled. (We always feel guilty doing that, but then again, we frequently mangle our fingers peeling those suckers.)

PREP TIME: 30 minutes
COOKING TIME: 2 hours on high or 4–5 hours on low
ADDITIONAL STEPS: Add the butter and mash the squash after cooking

INGREDIENTS

- **1 butternut squash (about 3 pounds or 1365 g)**

- Salt and pepper to taste

- **¹/₂ cup (115 g) light brown sugar**

- **1 teaspoon (2.3 g) ground cinnamon**

- 3 tablespoons (42 g) unsalted butter

Peel the squash and cut it in half lengthwise. Scoop out and discard the seeds and any pulp in the seed cavity. Cut the squash into 2- or 3-inch (5- or 7.5-cm) chunks and put into the slow cooker. Add salt and pepper to taste, ¹/₂ cup (120 ml) water, the brown sugar, and the cinnamon. Cook on high for 2 hours or on low for 4 to 5 hours, until the squash is quite soft. Add the butter and mash with a potato masher.

YIELD: *6 to 8 servings*

NUTRITIONAL ANALYSIS

137 calories; 4g fat (26.9% calories from fat); 1g protein; 26g carbohydrate; 3g dietary fiber; 12mg cholesterol; 53mg sodium.

🌸 Corn with Peppers and Onion

The colors in this dish are pretty and the taste delights.

PREP TIME: 15 minutes
COOKING TIME: 1¹/₂ hours on high or 3–4 hours on low

INGREDIENTS

- **1 pound (455 g) frozen corn**

- **1 medium-size onion**

- **1 bell pepper (red or orange)**

- 2 to 3 tablespoons (28 to 42 g) unsalted butter

- Salt and pepper to taste

Put the corn into the slow cooker. Peel and dice the onion into small pieces. Core the pepper and dice into ¹/₂-inch (1-cm) pieces. Add the onion and pepper to the corn and stir. Top with the butter and season with salt and pepper to taste. Cook for 1¹/₂ hours on high or 3 to 4 hours on low.

YIELD: *4 to 6 servings*

NUTRITIONAL ANALYSIS

130 calories; 6g fat (40.3% calories from fat); 3g protein; 19g carbohydrate; 2g dietary fiber; 16mg cholesterol; 62mg sodium.

✚ ADD IT IN!

Sprinkle a handful of chopped fresh cilantro over the corn before serving to create a bright trifecta of color.

✿ Creamed Jerusalem Artichokes

Also known as sunchokes, these tubers are the root of a sunflower plant and have a rich, mild flavor. This dish is perfect for when you want something a little different.

PREP TIME: 30 minutes
COOKING TIME: 2 hours on high or 5–6 hours on low

INGREDIENTS

- **1 pound (455 g) Jerusalem artichokes**
- **1 cup (245 g) Alfredo sauce**
- Salt and pepper to taste
- **1/2 cup (40 g) shredded Parmesan cheese**

Peel the Jerusalem artichokes and cut into 1-inch (2.5-cm) pieces. Put them into the slow cooker and add the Alfredo sauce along with salt and pepper to taste. Stir, then top with the Parmesan. Cook for 2 hours on high or 5 to 6 hours on low, until the chokes are tender.

YIELD: *4 servings*

NUTRITIONAL ANALYSIS

248 calories; 14g fat (49.0% calories from fat); 9g protein; 23g carbohydrate; 2g dietary fiber; 42mg cholesterol; 504mg sodium.

✚ ADD IT IN!

Try stirring some chopped fresh tarragon into this dish before cooking.

 Crumb-Topped Broccoli Bake

A wonderful side dish for fish or chicken, broccoli is generally a favorite with the small-fry, too.

PREP TIME: 15 minutes
COOKING TIME: 1^1/$_2$ hours on high or 3–4 hours on low

INGREDIENTS

- **1 bunch broccoli**

- **2 cups (490 g) Alfredo sauce**

- **1 cup (115 g) seasoned bread crumbs**

Cut up the broccoli, discarding the last 2 to 3 inches (5 to 7.5 cm) of the stem. Put the broccoli into the slow cooker and pour the Alfredo sauce over it. Sprinkle the crumbs on top and cook for 1^1/$_2$ hours on high or 3 to 4 hours on low.

YIELD: *4 servings*

NUTRITIONAL ANALYSIS

393 calories; 23g fat (51.2% calories from fat); 15g protein; 35g carbohydrate; 6g dietary fiber; 71 mg cholesterol; 1496mg sodium.

Cumin-Scented Spinach with Chickpeas

Cumin, an aromatic spice that is a favorite in Middle Eastern, Asian, and Mediterranean cooking, is a foundation spice with curries. Here, we use it to add kick to spinach.

PREP TIME: 20 minutes
COOKING TIME: 2 hours on high or 3–4 hours on low

INGREDIENTS

- **1 pound (455 g) fresh spinach**

- **1 (12-ounce or 340-g) can chickpeas (garbanzo beans)**

- **1 tablespoon (7 g) ground cumin**

- Salt and pepper to taste

- 2 tablespoons (28 g) unsalted butter

Wash the spinach and pick through it, removing grit, large stems, and any rotten leaves. Put the spinach into the slow cooker. Drain the chickpeas and add them to the slow cooker. Add the cumin and salt and pepper to taste. Stir to combine and dot with the butter. Cook for 2 hours on high or 3 to 4 hours on low. Stir and serve.

YIELD: *4 to 6 servings*

NUTRITIONAL ANALYSIS

261 calories; 8g fat (25.5% calories from fat); 13g protein; 37g carbohydrate; 12g dietary fiber; 10mg cholesterol; 114mg sodium.

 Curried Cauliflower

Use a good-quality curry powder to make this dish sing.

PREP TIME: 15 minutes

COOKING TIME: 2 hours on high or 5–6 hours on low

INGREDIENTS

- **1 head cauliflower**

- Salt and pepper to taste

- **1 medium-size onion**

- **1 tablespoon (7 g) curry powder**

Remove the outer leaves and the core from the cauliflower and cut it into florets. Put the florets into the slow cooker with salt and pepper to taste and $^1/_2$ cup (120 ml) water. Peel the onion and chop it into small dice. Add the onion and the curry powder to the slow cooker and stir. Cook on high for 2 hours or on low for 5 to 6 hours, until the cauliflower is tender.

YIELD: *4 to 6 servings*

NUTRITIONAL ANALYSIS

15 calories; trace fat (11.2% calories from fat); 1g protein; 3g carbohydrate; 1g dietary fiber; 0mg cholesterol; 6mg sodium.

🌸 Eggplant, Zucchini, and Tomato Layered Casserole

This casserole answers the annual late-summer question of what the heck to do with all those zucchinis and tomatoes once the neighbors start locking their doors when you knock.

PREP TIME: 30 minutes
COOKING TIME: 3 hours on high or 6–7 hours on low

INGREDIENTS

- **2 medium-size eggplants (about 2 pounds or 910 g)**

- **2 pounds (910 g) zucchini squash**

- **3 pounds (1365 g) tomatoes**

- Salt and pepper to taste

Peel the eggplants and slice them $^1/_2$ inch (1 cm) thick across. Trim the ends from the squash and slice them $^1/_2$ inch (1 cm) thick. Remove the core from the tomatoes and slice them $^1/_2$ inch (1 cm) thick across. Layer tomatoes on the bottom of the slow cooker, and top with a layer of eggplant, then zucchini. Season with salt and pepper, then repeat layers until the vegetables are used up, finishing with a layer of tomato. Cook for 3 hours on high or 6 to 7 hours on low. Serve right out of the slow cooker insert.

YIELD: *6 to 8 servings*

NUTRITIONAL ANALYSIS

77 calories; 1g fat (8.4% calories from fat); 4g protein; 17g carbohydrate; 6g dietary fiber; 0mg cholesterol; 21 mg sodium.

✚ ADD IT IN!

Sliced onion and minced garlic are flavor-enhancing additions.

 Eggplant, Basil, and Ricotta Bake

This hearty dish works nicely as a vegetarian entrée.

PREP TIME: 20 minutes
COOKING TIME: 3 hours on high or 6–7 hours on low

INGREDIENTS

- **2 large eggplants (about 3 pounds or 1365 g)**

- **1 cup (260 g) basil pesto**

- **2 cups (500 g) ricotta cheese**

- Salt and pepper to taste

Peel the eggplants and cut them into slices about ½ inch (1 cm) thick. Layer the bottom of the slow cooker with eggplant. Mix the pesto and ricotta together in a bowl with salt and pepper to taste. Spread some of the ricotta mixture on the eggplant in the slow cooker. Repeat layers, finishing with a layer of eggplant. Cook for 3 hours on high or 6 to 7 hours on low.

YIELD: *6 to 8 servings*

NUTRITIONAL ANALYSIS

289 calories; 22g fat (67.6% calories from fat); 13g protein; 11 g carbohydrate; 3g dietary fiber; 40mg cholesterol; 261 mg sodium.

✚ ADD IT IN!

Mix chopped fresh tomatoes in the pesto and ricotta to add another flavor layer.

 Endive Baked with Gruyère

We aren't sure whether this fits into the category of classics, but it sure is good. Endive yields a mild and deliciously nutty flavor that far outstrips its sharp, raw taste.

PREP TIME: 15 minutes
COOKING TIME: 2 hours on high or 5–6 hours on low

INGREDIENTS

- **4 heads Belgian endive**

- **1 cup (110 g) shredded Gruyère or other Swiss-type cheese**

- **2 tablespoons (5 g) minced fresh thyme**

- Salt and pepper to taste

Trim the root ends of the endive and split them lengthwise. Put the endive into the slow cooker and top with the cheese and thyme, along with salt and pepper to taste. Cook for 2 hours on high or 5 to 6 hours on low, until the endive is very soft and a little caramelized.

YIELD: *4 servings*

NUTRITIONAL ANALYSIS

202 calories; 10g fat (40.9% calories from fat); 15g protein; 18g carbohydrate; 16g dietary fiber; 30mg cholesterol; 205mg sodium.

 Maple Walnut Carrots

Sweet and earthy with the added crunch of the walnuts, these carrots make a delightful side dish for a holiday meal, or any day.

PREP TIME: 30 minutes
COOKING TIME: 3 hours on high or 5–6 hours on low

INGREDIENTS

- **2 pounds (910 g) carrots**
- **1 cup (340 g) maple syrup**
- 3 tablespoons (42 g) unsalted butter
- Salt and pepper to taste
- **1 cup (125 g) walnut pieces**

Peel the carrots and cut them into 2- or 3-inch (5- or 7.5-cm) pieces. Put the carrots into the slow cooker along with the maple syrup, the butter, $\frac{1}{2}$ cup (120 ml) water, and salt and pepper to taste. Sprinkle the walnuts over all and cook for 3 hours on high or 5 to 6 hours on low, until the carrots are tender. Stir.

YIELD: *4 to 6 servings*

NUTRITIONAL ANALYSIS

373 calories; 18g fat (41.0% calories from fat); 7g protein; 51 g carbohydrate; 5g dietary fiber; 16mg cholesterol; 111 mg sodium.

✚ ADD IT IN!

Toss the carrots with a little orange zest before serving.

Parsnip and Carrot Medley

If you've ever had parsnips that have stayed in the ground beyond the first frost, you know how sweet this delightful root can be. Here we capitalize on that sweetness, to the delight of parsnip fans everywhere.

PREP TIME: 30 minutes

COOKING TIME: 2 hours on high or 5–6 hours on low

INGREDIENTS

- **1 pound (455 g) carrots**

- **1 pound (455 g) parsnips**

- **1 teaspoon (2.2 g) nutmeg**

- Salt and pepper to taste

- 3 tablespoons (42 g) unsalted butter

Peel the carrots and the parsnips and cut them into 1-inch-long (2.5-cm) pieces. Put the vegetables into the slow cooker. Stir in the nutmeg and season with salt and pepper to taste. Add 1/2 cup (120 ml) water and dot with the butter. Cook for 2 hours on high or 5 to 6 hours on low, until the vegetables are tender.

YIELD: *4 to 6 servings*

NUTRITIONAL ANALYSIS

130 calories; 6g fat (40.9% calories from fat); 2g protein; 19g carbohydrate; 5g dietary fiber; 16mg cholesterol; 89mg sodium.

 Slow-Baked Fennel and Onions

Fennel and onions are two vegetables that are sharp when raw but become mellow and sweet when cooked slowly, as they are in this scrumptious dish.

PREP TIME: 20 minutes
COOKING TIME: 3 hours on high or 6–7 hours on low

INGREDIENTS

- **2 bulbs fennel**

- **1 pound (455 g) onions (3 or 4 medium-size)**

- ¹/₄ cup (60 ml) extra-virgin olive oil

- Salt and pepper to taste

- **1 cup (80 g) shredded Parmesan cheese**

Remove the stalks from the fennel and discard them. Trim away any discolored outer layers from the bulbs. Split the bulbs in half, lengthwise, and remove the core. Slice the fennel thin and put it into a mixing bowl. Peel the onions and slice them thin. Add the onions to the fennel and toss with the extra-virgin olive oil and salt and pepper to taste.

Put the fennel and onion mixture into the slow cooker and smooth out the top of the mixed veggies. Sprinkle the Parmesan cheese over the top. Cook on high for 3 hours or on low for 6 to 7 hours.

YIELD: *4 to 6 servings*

NUTRITIONAL ANALYSIS

185 calories; 13g fat (60.7% calories from fat); 7g protein; 12g carbohydrate; 4g dietary fiber; 10mg cholesterol; 269mg sodium.

 Mashed Turnips

Poor turnips have an undeserved reputation among the Young and Judgmental of being dull and gag-inducing, but these root veggies have a sweet, sharp taste that's really delightful. Here, we use cider to balance the sharp tang with more sweetness.

PREP TIME: 30 minutes
COOKING TIME: 2 hours on high or 4–5 hours on low
ADDITIONAL STEPS: Mash the turnips after cooking

INGREDIENTS

- **2 pounds (910 g) turnips**

- **½ cup (120 ml) apple cider**

- **1 teaspoon (2.3 g) ground coriander**

- Salt and pepper to taste

- 2 tablespoons (28 g) unsalted butter

Peel the turnips and cut them into 1-inch (2.5-cm) cubes. Put the turnips into the slow cooker and add the cider and coriander, along with salt and pepper to taste. Cook for 2 hours on high or 4 to 5 hours on low. Add the butter and mash the turnips with a potato masher.

YIELD: *6 to 8 servings*

NUTRITIONAL ANALYSIS

58 calories; 3g fat (44.3% calories from fat); 1g protein; 8g carbohydrate; 2g dietary fiber; 8mg cholesterol; 91 mg sodium.

 Stewed Butterbeans

Also known as lima beans, these big, meaty beans deserve a better reputation than they have. (Our sister still refers to them as "little sandbags" and creates bean barricades on her plate when they appear—setting a bad example for her children, we might add.) Try this dish and we know you'll be on our side!

PREP TIME: 10 minutes

COOKING TIME: 2 hours on high or 4–5 hours on low

INGREDIENTS

- **1 pound (455 g) frozen butter beans or large lima beans**

- **1 medium-size onion**

- **1 cup (180 g) diced fresh tomato**

- Salt and pepper to taste

Put the butter beans into the slow cooker. Peel the onion and cut it into small dice. Add the onion and the diced tomato and season with salt and pepper to taste. Stir and cover. Cook on high for 2 hours or on low for 4 to 5 hours.

YIELD: *4 servings*

NUTRITIONAL ANALYSIS

170 calories; 1g fat (3.5% calories from fat); 9g protein; 33g carbohydrate; 6g dietary fiber; 0mg cholesterol; 64mg sodium.

> ✚ ADD IT IN!
>
> Spice it up with a couple of cloves of minced garlic.

 # Stewed Greens

This Southern staple is perfect for the slow cooker. The liquid, known as the "pot likker," makes a great dip for your cornbread.

PREP TIME: 20 minutes
COOKING TIME: 3 hours on high or 6–7 hours on low

INGREDIENTS

- **1 bunch greens, such as collards, mustard greens, or kale**

- **3 strips bacon**

- **¼ cup (60 ml) apple cider vinegar**

- Salt and pepper to taste

Strip out the large stems from the greens and wash them thoroughly. Chop the greens and put them into the slow cooker. Chop the bacon into small pieces and add it to the greens. Add the vinegar, salt and pepper to taste, and 2 cups (470 ml) water. Cook on high for 3 hours or on low for 6 to 7 hours. Serve in bowls with some of the cooking liquid.

 SERVING SUGGESTION: *This is traditionally served with a square of cornbread.*

YIELD: *4 servings*

NUTRITIONAL ANALYSIS

32 calories; 2g fat (63.4% calories from fat); 2g protein; 1g carbohydrate; trace dietary fiber; 4mg cholesterol; 78mg sodium.

Stewed Mushrooms with Garlic and Tarragon

Here's a spectacular side dish for your roast or steak. Find some nice small button mushrooms that you can leave whole and you'll be good to go.

PREP TIME: 10 minutes

COOKING TIME: 2 hours on high or 3–4 hours on low

ADDITIONAL STEPS: Stir in the tarragon during the last few minutes of cooking

INGREDIENTS

- **1 pound (455 g) small button mushrooms**

- **1 tablespoon (10 g) minced garlic**

- Salt and pepper to taste

- **3 tablespoons (7 g) minced fresh tarragon**

Rinse the mushrooms only if they are dirty; otherwise, do not wash them. Trim the stems and put the mushrooms into the slow cooker. Add the garlic and salt and pepper to taste. Cook on high for 2 hours or on low for 3 to 4 hours. Stir in the tarragon and cook for a few more minutes.

YIELD: *4 servings*

NUTRITIONAL ANALYSIS

41 calories; 1g fat (10.6% calories from fat); 3g protein; 8g carbohydrate; 2g dietary fiber; 0mg cholesterol; 7mg sodium.

 Summer Stewed Tomatoes

This recipe is another great way to use the bounty of your (or your local farmer's) harvest. We always run amok when the tomatoes come in, as our New England winter is so very long, and grocery store tomatoes—although much improved—still aren't the same as garden-fresh.

PREP TIME: 20 minutes

COOKING TIME: 3 hours on high or 6–7 hours on low

INGREDIENTS

- **3 pounds (1365 g) ripe tomatoes**

- **2 tablespoons (20 g) minced garlic**

- **1/2 cup (20 g) shredded fresh basil**

- Salt and pepper to taste

Core the tomatoes and cut them into wedges. Put the tomatoes into the slow cooker and add the garlic and basil, along with salt and pepper to taste. Stir gently. Cook for 3 hours on high or 6 to 7 hours on low.

SERVING SUGGESTION: *Cook up a pot of pasta and toss this on as a delicious summer sauce.*

YIELD: *4 to 6 servings*

NUTRITIONAL ANALYSIS

49 calories; 1 g fat (11.1 % calories from fat); 2g protein; 11 g carbohydrate; 2g dietary fiber; 0mg cholesterol; 19mg sodium.

CHAPTER 9

POTATOES, GRAINS, AND BEANS

Most people think of entrées when they think of slow cooking, but slow cookers are equally handy for side dishes such as potatoes, rice and other grains, and beans and other dried legumes (such as lentils). Using a slow cooker for the scalloped potatoes at Easter frees up an entire rack in the oven, and it also means that the harried cook can cross that food item off his or her "To Do" list before the real crunch time of food prep and service kicks in. Slow cookers also let summer cooks use the grill for the meat while cooking the starch in a slow cooker, which puts out far less heat than the stove or oven. All in all, these recipes prove that a slow cooker is far more than a one-dish pony.

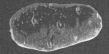

Au Gratin Potatoes

This rich and cheesy classic works beautifully as a side dish at a holiday meal, and the slow cooker frees up precious stove and oven space.

PREP TIME: 30 minutes
COOKING TIME: 2^1/$_2$–3 hours on high or 6–7 hours on low

INGREDIENTS

- **4 or 5 large baking potatoes, such as russet**

- Nonstick cooking spray

- Salt and pepper to taste

- **2^1/$_2$ cups (300 g) grated sharp cheddar cheese**

- **2 cups (470 ml) milk or half-and-half**

Peel the potatoes and cut them into ^{1}/$_8$- to ^{1}/$_4$-inch-thick (3- to 6-mm) rounds. Spray the bottom and side of the slow cooker with the nonstick cooking spray. Put a layer of potatoes on the bottom of the slow cooker. Season with salt and pepper and sprinkle with some of the cheese. Repeat layers with the remaining ingredients, ending with a layer of cheese. Pour the milk over all. Cook for 2^1/$_2$ to 3 hours on high or 6 to 7 hours on low.

YIELD: *6 servings*

NUTRITIONAL ANALYSIS

361 calories; 19g fat (45.7% calories from fat); 18g protein; 32g carbohydrate; 2g dietary fiber; 61 mg cholesterol; 342mg sodium.

✚ ADD IT IN!

Add in ^{1}/$_2$ cup (80 g) chopped onions to the potato layers for extra tang.

Creamed Potato and Celery Root

Celery root, also known as celeriac, is one of the more unprepossessing vegetables out there, but this gnarly lump of a vegetable has a delicate and distinctive flavor that we love. You won't be sorry that you've added this to your cuisine— it's perfectly matched with poultry or veal.

PREP TIME: 30 minutes
COOKING TIME: 3 hours on high or 6–7 hours on low

INGREDIENTS

- **2 pounds (910 g) celery root**

- **3 pounds (1365 g) potatoes**

- Salt and pepper to taste

- **1 cup (235 ml) light cream**

Thoroughly wash the celery root and potatoes. Peel them (with celery root, you will most easily accomplish this task with a knife) and cut them both into $1/2$-inch (1-cm) cubes. Put the potatoes and celery root into the slow cooker. Season with salt and pepper to taste. Pour the cream over them and cook for 3 hours on high or 6 to 7 hours on low. Stir to redistribute the cream and serve.

YIELD: *6 to 8 servings*

NUTRITIONAL ANALYSIS

211 calories; 6g fat (25.1 % calories from fat); 5g protein; 36g carbohydrate; 5g dietary fiber; 20mg cholesterol; 121mg sodium.

Mashed Potatoes with Scallions

PREP TIME: 30 minutes

COOKING TIME: 2 1/2 hours on high

ADDITIONAL STEPS: Mash the potatoes after cooking, adding the milk and scallions

INGREDIENTS

- **3 pounds (1365 g) potatoes**

- Salt and pepper to taste

- **1 cup (235 ml) milk**

- **1 cup (100 g) chopped scallions**

- 2 tablespoons (28 g) unsalted butter

Wash and peel the potatoes. Cut them into 1-inch (2.5-cm) cubes. Put the potatoes into the slow cooker and season with salt and pepper to taste. Add 2 cups (470 ml) water. Cook on high for 2 1/2 hours, until the potatoes are tender. Drain off most of the water. Mash the potatoes in the slow cooker with a potato masher. Stir in the milk, scallions, and butter.

YIELD: *6 servings*

NUTRITIONAL ANALYSIS

209 calories; 2g fat (6.7% calories from fat); 6g protein; 44g carbohydrate; 4g dietary fiber; 6mg cholesterol; 36mg sodium.

New Potatoes with Dill

Adding the dill at the last minute keeps it nice and green, and lends a flavor explosion.

PREP TIME: 10 minutes
COOKING TIME: 2 hours on high or 3–4 hours on low
ADDITIONAL STEPS: Add the chopped dill at the end

INGREDIENTS

- **3 pounds (1365 g) baby new potatoes**

- Salt and pepper to taste

- 2 tablespoons (28 g) unsalted butter

- **2 tablespoons (8 g) chopped fresh dill**

Wash the potatoes and put them into the slow cooker. Season with salt and pepper to taste. Add 2 cups (470 ml) water and the butter. Cook on high for 2 hours or on low for 3 to 4 hours. Remove the potatoes from the cooker with a slotted spoon and put them into a bowl.

Stir the dill into the potatoes and serve.

YIELD: *4 to 6 servings*

NUTRITIONAL ANALYSIS

213 calories; 4g fat (16.7% calories from fat); 5g protein; 41 g carbohydrate; 4g dietary fiber; 10mg cholesterol; 53mg sodium.

New Potatoes with Garlic and Parsley

Slow-cooked garlic and fresh parsley add a nice kick to everybody's favorite starch.

PREP TIME: 10 minutes
COOKING TIME: 2 hours on high or 3–4 hours on low
ADDITIONAL STEPS: Add the chopped parsley at the end

INGREDIENTS

- **3 pounds (1365 g) baby new potatoes**

- Salt and pepper to taste

- **6 to 8 cloves garlic, peeled**

- 2 tablespoons (30 ml) extra-virgin olive oil

- **2 tablespoons (8 g) chopped fresh parsley**

Wash the potatoes and put them into the slow cooker. Season with salt and pepper to taste. Add 2 cups (470 ml) water, the garlic, and the olive oil. Cook on high for 2 hours or on low for 3 to 4 hours. Remove the potatoes from the cooker with a slotted spoon and put them into a bowl.

Stir the parsley into the potatoes.

YIELD: *4 to 6 servings*

NUTRITIONAL ANALYSIS

226 calories; 5g fat (18.5% calories from fat); 5g protein; 42g carbohydrate; 4g dietary fiber; 0mg cholesterol; 15mg sodium.

 Potato and Sauerkraut Bake

If you can find it, use the fresh-pack sauerkraut found in the refrigerated section (usually near the hot dogs)—it's got much more flavor than the canned variety. This is really nice with brats at a summer cookout.

PREP TIME: 30 minutes
COOKING TIME: 3 hours on high or 5–6 hours on low
ADDITIONAL STEPS: Rinse the sauerkraut

INGREDIENTS

- **1 pound (455 g) sauerkraut**

- **3 pounds (1365 g) potatoes**

- Pepper to taste

- **1 cup (230 g) sour cream**

Put the sauerkraut into a colander and rinse well under cold water. Peel the potatoes and slice into ¹/₄-inch-thick (6-mm) rounds.

Put a layer of sauerkraut on the bottom of the slow cooker and top with a layer of potatoes. Season with pepper to taste (the kraut is already salty). Repeat with the remaining sauerkraut and potatoes. Cook for 3 hours on high or 5 to 6 hours on low. Serve with a dollop of sour cream on top.

YIELD: *6 servings*

NUTRITIONAL ANALYSIS

276 calories; 8g fat (26.5% calories from fat); 7g protein; 46g carbohydrate; 6g dietary fiber; 17mg cholesterol; 534mg sodium.

✚ ADD IT IN!

Sprinkle the top with caraway seeds for extra flavor.

Potatoes with Peppers and Onions

This is a great recipe for a summer cookout, especially if you're sick of over-mayonnaised macaroni or potato salad. Try serving this with grilled fish or chicken. Use different-colored peppers to pack a visual punch.

PREP TIME: 30 minutes
COOKING TIME: 3 hours on high or 5–6 hours on low

INGREDIENTS

- **4 pounds (1820 g) potatoes**

- **2 medium-size onions (about 1 pound or 455 g)**

- **2 medium-size bell peppers, any colors (about 1 pound or 455 g)**

- Salt and pepper to taste

- 2 to 3 tablespoons (30 to 45 ml) extra-virgin olive oil

Wash and peel the potatoes and slice them into ¼-inch-thick (6-mm) rounds. Peel the onions and slice them ¼ inch (6 mm) thick. Core the peppers and cut them into rings.

Layer some of the potatoes in the slow cooker and season with salt and pepper. Add a layer of some of the onions and peppers. Repeat layers with the remaining ingredients. Pour the olive oil and ½ cup (120 ml) of water over all and cook for 3 hours on high or 5 to 6 hours on low.

YIELD: *6 servings*

NUTRITIONAL ANALYSIS

323 calories; 7g fat (19.4% calories from fat); 7g protein; 60g carbohydrate; 6g dietary fiber; 0mg cholesterol; 20mg sodium.

Scalloped Potatoes

This is the classic home-style dish, and the perfect match for that baked ham.

PREP TIME: 30 minutes
COOKING TIME: 3–4 hours on high or 7–8 hours on low

INGREDIENTS

- **5 pounds (2275 g) potatoes**

- Salt and pepper to taste

- 4 tablespoons ($^1/_2$ stick or 55 g) unsalted butter

- **$^1/_2$ cup (60 g) all-purpose flour**

- **2 cups (470 ml) milk**

Peel the potatoes and cut them into $^1/_4$-inch-thick (6-mm) rounds. Put a layer of potatoes on the bottom of the slow cooker. Season with salt and pepper and dot with a little butter. Sprinkle 1 tablespoon (8 g) flour over the potatoes. Repeat layers with the remaining ingredients. Pour the milk over the potatoes. Cook for 3 to 4 hours on high or 7 to 8 hours on low.

YIELD: *6 servings*

NUTRITIONAL ANALYSIS

455 calories; 11 g fat (21.1 % calories from fat); 12g protein; 80g carbohydrate; 6g dietary fiber; 32mg cholesterol; 141mg sodium.

Scalloped Potatoes with Bacon

PREP TIME: 30 minutes

COOKING TIME: 3–4 hours on high or 7–8 hours on low

INGREDIENTS

- **5 pounds (2275 g) potatoes**

- **1/2 pound (230 g) cooked bacon**

- Salt and pepper to taste

- **1 cup (235 ml) chicken stock or broth**

Peel the potatoes and cut them into 1/4-inch-thick (6-mm) rounds. Chop the bacon into small pieces. Put a layer of potatoes on the bottom of the slow cooker. Season with salt and pepper and scatter some of the bacon over the potatoes. Repeat layers with the remaining potatoes and bacon. Pour the stock over the potatoes. Cook for 3 to 4 hours on high or 7 to 8 hours on low.

YIELD: *6 servings*

NUTRITIONAL ANALYSIS

520 calories; 19g fat (32.7% calories from fat); 19g protein; 68g carbohydrate; 6g dietary fiber; 32mg cholesterol; 984mg sodium.

+ ADD IT IN!

Sprinkle some crumbled dried rosemary among the layers.

 Baked Potatoes

Why heat a big oven for baked potatoes? The slow cooker does a great job.

PREP TIME: 10 minutes
COOKING TIME: 2 hours on high or 4–5 hours on low

INGREDIENTS

- **6 baking potatoes (about 5 pounds or 2275 g)**

- Salt and pepper to taste

Wash the potatoes and stick each of them with a knife. Put the potatoes into the slow cooker and season with salt and pepper. Cook for 2 hours on high or 4 to 5 hours on low.

YIELD: *6 servings*

NUTRITIONAL ANALYSIS

145 calories; trace fat (1.1% calories from fat); 4g protein; 33g carbohydrate; 3g dietary fiber; 0mg cholesterol; 11 mg sodium.

Cheesy Mashed Potatoes

This is an easy way to make great mashed potatoes.

PREP TIME: 30 minutes

COOKING TIME: 2 ¹/₂ hours on high

ADDITIONAL STEPS: Mash the potatoes after cooking; add the milk and cheese

INGREDIENTS

- **3 pounds (1365 g) potatoes**

- Salt and pepper to taste

- **1 cup (235 ml) milk**

- **1 cup (115 g) shredded cheddar cheese**

- 2 tablespoons (28 g) unsalted butter

Wash and peel the potatoes and cut them into 1-inch (2.5-cm) cubes. Put the potatoes into the slow cooker and season with salt and pepper to taste. Add 2 cups (470 ml) water and cook on high for 2 ¹/₂ hours. Drain off most of the water and mash the potatoes in the slow cooker with a potato masher. Stir in the milk. Stir in the cheese and butter until melted.

YIELD: *6 servings*

NUTRITIONAL ANALYSIS

280 calories; 8g fat (24.7% calories from fat); 11 g protein; 43g carbohydrate; 4g dietary fiber; 25mg cholesterol; 150mg sodium.

 Almond Rice

The almonds in this dish add a subtle crunch. You'll find that converted rice works well in a slow cooker if you like the grains separate.

PREP TIME: 20 minutes
COOKING TIME: 3 hours on high or 5–6 hours on low
ADDITIONAL STEPS: Toast the almonds

INGREDIENTS

- **1 cup (92 g) sliced blanched almonds**

- **3 cups (585 g) converted rice**

- **3 cups (705 g) chicken stock or broth**

- Salt and pepper to taste

Preheat the oven to 350°F (180°C or gas mark 4). Spread the almonds on a cookie sheet and bake for 10 to 12 minutes, until golden brown. Put the rice into the slow cooker. Stir in the almonds. Add the stock and 3 cups (705 ml) water. Season with salt and pepper to taste. Cook for 3 hours on high or 5 to 6 hours on low, until the liquid is absorbed and the rice is tender.

YIELD: *8 to 10 servings*

NUTRITIONAL ANALYSIS

296 calories; 8g fat (23.4% calories from fat); 8g protein; 49g carbohydrate; 1g dietary fiber; 0mg cholesterol; 646mg sodium. Exchanges: 3 Grain(Starch); $1/2$ Lean Meat; $1^1/2$ Fat.

 Coconut Rice

A favorite accompaniment in island cuisines, this dish has a distinctive flavor that makes it a terrific match for many kinds of grilled fish. Add a fruit salsa and enjoy!

PREP TIME: 10 minutes
COOKING TIME: 3 hours on high or 5–6 hours on low
ADDITIONAL STEPS: Stir in the chives just before serving

INGREDIENTS

- **3 cups (585 g) converted rice**

- **1 (12-ounce or 355-ml) can coconut milk**

- Salt and pepper to taste

- **¼ cup (12 g) chopped fresh chives**

Put the rice into the slow cooker. Stir in the coconut milk. Add 4 cups (940 ml) water. Season with salt and pepper to taste. Cook for 3 hours on high or 5 to 6 hours on low, until the liquid is absorbed and the rice is tender. Stir in the chives.

YIELD: *8 to 10 servings*

NUTRITIONAL ANALYSIS

283 calories; 8g fat (25.6% calories from fat); 6g protein; 48g carbohydrate; 1g dietary fiber; 0mg cholesterol; 5mg sodium.

 Curried Rice

This kicky rice dish is a diverting summer side with grilled chicken and vegetable kabobs.

PREP TIME: 10 minutes
COOKING TIME: 3 hours on high or 5–6 hours on low

INGREDIENTS

- **3 cups (585 g) converted rice**

- **1 cup (165 g) golden raisins**

- **2 tablespoons (15 g) curry powder**

- Salt and pepper to taste

Put the rice into the slow cooker. Stir in the raisins and curry powder. Add 5 cups (1200 ml) water. Season with salt and pepper to taste. Cook for 3 hours on high or 5 to 6 hours on low, until the liquid is absorbed and the rice is tender.

YIELD: *8 to 10 servings*

NUTRITIONAL ANALYSIS

252 calories; trace fat (0.8% calories from fat); 5g protein; 58g carbohydrate; 1g dietary fiber; 0mg cholesterol; 2mg sodium.

Easy Risotto

This no-muss, no-fuss version of risotto does away with the tedious stirring and adding of liquid that's necessary with stovetop risottos. The result is a nice, creamy risotto. Buy a chunk of fresh Parmesan and grate it yourself—it really does taste better than the stuff in the green can.

PREP TIME: 10 minutes

COOKING TIME: 1 hour

ADDITIONAL STEPS: Stir in the Parmesan cheese at the end

INGREDIENTS

- **2 cups (390 g) Arborio rice**

- ¹/₄ cup (60 ml) extra-virgin olive oil

- **1 cup (235 ml) light cream**

- Salt and pepper to taste

Put the rice into the slow cooker with the olive oil. Turn on the cooker to high and cook the rice, stirring occasionally, for 15 to 20 minutes, until the rice is a little translucent around the edges. Add the cream and 2¹/₂ cups (590 ml) water. Season with salt and pepper to taste. Reduce the heat to low and cook for 30 to 40 minutes, until the liquid is almost absorbed and the rice is tender on the outside and just slightly chewy on the inside (al dente). Stir in the Parmesan cheese.

YIELD: *6 to 8 servings*

NUTRITIONAL ANALYSIS

228 calories; 10g fat (40.3% calories from fat); 3g protein; 30g carbohydrate; 0g dietary fiber; 16mg cholesterol; 16mg sodium.

✚ ADD IT IN!

You can substitute white wine and/or chicken stock for the water. As with any risotto, this basic recipe can be used as a base for many additions, such as mushrooms, peas, shellfish, saffron—the list goes on.

Easy Spanish Rice

A nice side dish or burrito filling, this is a good way to spice up the daily starch.

PREP TIME: 20 minutes
COOKING TIME: 3 hours on high or 5–6 hours on low

INGREDIENTS

- **3 cups (585 g) converted rice**

- **1 (12-ounce or 395-g) can diced tomatoes with peppers and onions**

- **2 tablespoons (15 g) chili powder**

- Salt and pepper to taste

Put the rice into the slow cooker. Add the tomatoes and 4 cups (940 ml) water. Stir in the chili powder. Season with salt and pepper to taste. Cook for 3 hours on high or 5 to 6 hours on low, until the liquid is absorbed and the rice is tender.

YIELD: *8 to 10 servings*

NUTRITIONAL ANALYSIS

216 calories; trace fat (1.5% calories from fat); 5g protein; 48g carbohydrate; 1g dietary fiber; 0mg cholesterol; 18mg sodium.

✚ ADD IT IN!

You can spice up this dish with whatever kind of hot chile or hot sauce appeals most to you.

 Mushroom Rice

*The rich, earthy flavor of the mushrooms and the deep flavor of the beef broth
make this a side dish you will use often. It's great with lamb chops or steak.*

PREP TIME: 10 minutes

COOKING TIME: 3 hours on high or 5–6 hours on low

ADDITIONAL STEPS: Sauté the mushrooms before adding to the slow cooker

INGREDIENTS

- 1 tablespoon (15 ml) cooking oil

- **2 cups (140 g) sliced mushrooms**

- **3 cups (585 g) converted rice**

- **3 cups (705 ml) beef stock or broth**

- Salt and pepper to taste

Heat a sauté pan over medium-high heat. Add the oil and sauté the mushrooms until they release their liquid.

Put the rice into the slow cooker. Stir in the mushrooms. Add the stock and
2 cups (470 ml) water. Season with salt and pepper to taste. Cook for 3
hours on high or 5 to 6 hours on low, until the liquid is absorbed and the
rice is tender.

YIELD: *6 to 8 servings*

NUTRITIONAL ANALYSIS

226 calories; 1g fat (6.0% calories from fat); 5g protein; 46g carbohydrate; trace
dietary fiber; 0mg cholesterol; 638mg sodium.

Lemon Ginger Rice

This sophisticated dish has a clean, crisp flavor that goes well with fish, chicken, or pork.

PREP TIME: 20 minutes
COOKING TIME: 3 hours on high or 5–6 hours on low
ADDITIONAL STEPS: Grate the lemon zest; juice the lemons; peel and mince the ginger

INGREDIENTS

- **2 lemons**

- **1 tablespoon (6 g) minced fresh ginger root**

- **3 cups (585 g) converted rice**

- Salt and pepper to taste

Grate the lemon zest, and then juice the lemons. Peel and mince the ginger.

Put the rice into the slow cooker. Stir in the lemon zest and juice. Stir in the ginger. Add 5 cups (1175 ml) water. Season with salt and pepper to taste. Cook for 3 hours on high or 5 to 6 hours on low, until the liquid is absorbed and the rice is tender.

YIELD: *8 to 10 servings*

NUTRITIONAL ANALYSIS

207 calories; trace fat (0.2% calories from fat); 5g protein; 47g carbohydrate; trace dietary fiber; 0mg cholesterol; trace sodium.

 # Pecan Wild Rice Pilaf

This dish is so good with roast chicken or turkey, and it's not bad with ham either!

PREP TIME: 10 minutes (40 mintues if rice isn't already par-cooked)
COOKING TIME: 3 hours on high or 5–6 hours on low
ADDITIONAL STEPS: Par-cook the wild rice

INGREDIENTS

- **1 cup (165 g) par-cooked wild rice (see note below)**

- **2 cups (390 g) converted rice**

- Salt and pepper to taste

- **1 cup (100 g) chopped pecans**

Note: To par-cook wild rice, place the wild rice in a saucepan and add enough water to cover the rice by 3 to 4 inches. Bring to a boil over medium-high heat and then reduce the heat to medium-low. Cook at a low boil for 30 minutes. Drain the rice and proceed with the recipe. You can also purchase wild rice already par-cooked.

Put the par-cooked wild rice and the converted rice into the slow cooker. Add 6 cups (1410 ml) water and season with salt and pepper. Stir in the pecans. Cook for 3 hours on high or 5 to 6 hours on low, until the water is absorbed and the rice is tender.

YIELD: *8 to 10 servings*

NUTRITIONAL ANALYSIS

232 calories; 8g fat (30.9% calories from fat); 5g protein; 36g carbohydrate; 1g dietary fiber; 0mg cholesterol; 1mg sodium.

+ ADD IT IN!

Stir in 2 tablespoons (28 g) unsalted butter and 1 tablespoon (5 g) chopped fresh sage just before serving.

 Rice Pilaf

This is the classic rice pilaf with toasted orzo pasta. It's easy and elegant in the slow cooker.

PREP TIME: 30 minutes
COOKING TIME: 2 hours on high or 4–5 hours on low
ADDITIONAL STEPS: Toast the orzo before adding to the slow cooker

INGREDIENTS

- 2 tablespoons (30 ml) cooking oil

- **1 cup (185 g) orzo**

- **2 cups (390 g) converted rice**

- **1 medium-size onion**

- Salt and pepper to taste

Heat a sauté pan over medium heat. Add the oil and then add the orzo. Cook, stirring often, until the orzo is golden brown.

Put the orzo into the slow cooker and add the rice. Chop the onion into small dice and add to the slow cooker. Season with salt and pepper to taste. Add 5 cups (1175 ml) water and stir. Cook for 2 hours on high or 4 to 5 hours on low, until the water is absorbed and the rice is tender.

YIELD: *8 to 10 servings*

NUTRITIONAL ANALYSIS

283 calories; 4g fat (12.1% calories from fat); 7g protein; 55g carbohydrate; 1g dietary fiber; 0mg cholesterol; 2mg sodium.

✚ ADD IT IN!

Our mom is very fond of serving rice pilaf at big family gatherings, and she always puts chopped celery in. We concur—why not try it here?

Saffron Rice with Dried Cranberries

Saffron is one of our favorite spices, just because of what it is: Who the heck ever thought that plucking the yellow stigmas from crocuses would add a taste sensation to his or her cooking? It undoubtedly does, however, so we applaud such creativity. Some cooks like to toast their saffron lightly in a sauté pan before adding it to the rice.

PREP TIME: 10 minutes
COOKING TIME: 2 hours on high or 5–6 hours on low

INGREDIENTS

- **3 cups (585 g) converted rice**

- **½ teaspoon saffron**

- **1 cup (120 g) dried cranberries**

- Salt and pepper to taste

Put the rice into the slow cooker. Stir in the saffron and cranberries. Add 5 cups (1175 ml) water. Season with salt and pepper to taste. Cook for 2 hours on high or 5 to 6 hours on low, until the liquid is absorbed and the rice is tender.

YIELD: *8 to 10 servings*

NUTRITIONAL ANALYSIS

205 calories; trace fat (0.0% calories from fat); 5g protein; 46g carbohydrate; trace dietary fiber; 0mg cholesterol; trace sodium.

Barley with Porcini Mushrooms

Dried porcini mushrooms taste wonderful, and their soaking liquid is used as a flavorful stock, letting us double down on flavor by doubling the effectiveness of one ingredient.

PREP TIME: 30 minutes
COOKING TIME: 2 hours on high or 4–5 hours on low
ADDITIONAL STEPS: Steep the porcini before adding to the slow cooker

INGREDIENTS

- **2 ounces (about 2 cups or 55 g) dried porcini mushrooms**
- **1 medium-size onion**
- **1 pound (455 g) pearl barley**
- Salt and pepper to taste

Bring 4 cups (940 ml) water to a boil. Put the porcini into a large bowl and pour the boiling water over them. Allow to steep for 20 minutes.

Peel the onion and chop it into small dice. Put the onion, the barley, and the porcini, along with the soaking liquid, into the slow cooker. Season with salt and pepper. Cook for 2 hours on high or 4 to 5 hours on low, until the water is absorbed and the barley is tender.

YIELD: *6 to 8 servings*

NUTRITIONAL ANALYSIS

226 calories; 1g fat (2.8% calories from fat); 6g protein; 51 g carbohydrate; 10g dietary fiber; 0mg cholesterol; 6mg sodium.

> **+ ADD IT IN!**
>
> Add some chopped fresh oregano to the mixture.

 # Kasha

Kasha, or buckwheat, has an unforgettable flavor that is quite addictive.

PREP TIME: 30 minutes
COOKING TIME: 2 hours on high or 3–4 hours on low

INGREDIENTS

- **1 (1-pound or 455-g) box medium kasha**

- **2 eggs**

- **3 cups (705 ml) chicken stock or broth**

Put the kasha into the slow cooker. Turn on the cooker to high. Break the eggs into a bowl and whisk lightly. Add to the kasha and stir until the grains are coated. Cook for 15 to 20 minutes on high, stirring every few minutes, then add the stock. Cover and cook for another $1^1/_2$ hours on high or turn to low and cook for 3 to 4 hours. The kasha is done when it is tender and the liquid is absorbed.

YIELD: *4 to 6 servings*

NUTRITIONAL ANALYSIS

292 calories; 4g fat (12.2% calories from fat); 12g protein; 55g carbohydrate; 8g dietary fiber; 62mg cholesterol; 1093mg sodium.

Minted Bulgur Wheat

With its nutty flavor and chewy texture, bulgur wheat is a great match for kebabs—or anything off the grill, for that matter. (We are on a mission to make the slow cooker your favorite grilling companion, because it keeps the kitchen cool!)

PREP TIME: 15 minutes
COOKING TIME: 2 hours on high or 3–4 hours on low
ADDITIONAL STEPS: Stir in the mint at the end

INGREDIENTS

- **1 pound (455 g) bulgur wheat**

- **1 medium-size onion**

- Salt and pepper to taste

- **¹/₂ cup (48 g) finely chopped fresh mint**

Put the bulgur wheat into the slow cooker. Peel the onion and cut it into small dice. Add the onion, and season with salt and pepper to taste. Add 4 cups (940 ml) water and cook for 2 hours on high or 3 to 4 hours on low, until the bulgur wheat is tender and the water is absorbed.

Stir the chopped mint into the bulgur and serve.

YIELD: *4 to 6 servings*

NUTRITIONAL ANALYSIS

269 calories; 1g fat (3.4% calories from fat); 10g protein; 60g carbohydrate; 15g dietary fiber; 0mg cholesterol; 16mg sodium.

 Cheese Grits

Grits have pretty much been relegated to the breakfast table, but these are crowd-pleasers any time of day. Try them as a side at dinner—they taste great with so many partners.

PREP TIME: 20 minutes

COOKING TIME: 2 hours on high or 3–4 hours on low

ADDITIONAL STEPS: Boil the water before adding to the slow cooker; stir in the cheese at the end

INGREDIENTS

- Butter or nonstick cooking spray

- **2 cups (275 g) grits (not instant)**

- Salt and pepper to taste

- **1 teaspoon (5 g) hot sauce**

- **2 cups (225 g) shredded cheddar cheese**

Butter the sides of the slow cooker. Put the grits into the slow cooker and stir in salt and pepper to taste. Turn on the slow cooker to high or low, as your prefer.

Put 4 cups (940 ml) water into a saucepan and bring to a boil. Stir the boiling water into the grits in the slow cooker, along with the hot sauce. Cook for 2 hours on high or 3 to 4 hours on low, until the liquid is absorbed and the grits are creamy. Stir in the cheese.

YIELD: *4 to 6 servings*

NUTRITIONAL ANALYSIS

345 calories; 13g fat (34.6% calories from fat); 14g protein; 42g carbohydrate; trace dietary fiber; 40mg cholesterol; 255mg sodium.

 Polenta

This is a sophisticated dish that's a welcome change from the usual starches. Serve this soft straight from the slow cooker, or cool, slice, and fry or grill.

PREP TIME: 20 minutes

COOKING TIME: 2 hours on high or 3–4 hours on low

ADDITIONAL STEPS: Boil the liquids before adding to the slow cooker; stir in the cheese at the end.

INGREDIENTS

- **2 cups (275 g) cornmeal (medium to coarse is best)**
- Salt and pepper to taste
- **2 cups (470 ml) milk**
- **1 cup (100 g) grated Parmesan cheese**

Put the cornmeal into the slow cooker and stir in salt and pepper to taste. Turn on the slow cooker to high or low, as you prefer.

Put the milk and 2 cups (470 ml) water into a saucepan and bring to a boil.

Stir the liquid into the cornmeal. Cook for 2 hours on high or 3 to 4 hours on low, until the liquid is absorbed and the polenta is creamy. Stir in the cheese and serve.

YIELD: *4 to 6 servings*

NUTRITIONAL ANALYSIS

279 calories; 7g fat (24.4% calories from fat); 12g protein; 40g carbohydrate; 3g dietary fiber; 22mg cholesterol; 289mg sodium.

BBQ Red Beans

Use your preferred barbecue sauce in this dish for an easy family favorite.

PREP TIME: 15 minutes
COOKING TIME: 1 hour on high or 3–4 hours on low.

INGREDIENTS

- **2 (14-ounce or 395-g) can red beans, such as kidney beans**

- **2 cups (500 g) barbecue sauce**

- **1 medium-size onion**

Drain the beans and put them into the slow cooker. Add the barbecue sauce. Peel the onion, chop into small dice, and add to the cooker. Cook for 1 hour on high or 3 to 4 hours on low. Stir.

YIELD: *6 to 8 servings*

NUTRITIONAL ANALYSIS

134 calories; 1g fat (10.2% calories from fat); 6g protein; 23g carbohydrate; 6g dietary fiber; 0mg cholesterol; 782mg sodium.

Black-Eyed Peas

Serve these delicious peas with some tender stewed greens and cornbread for a simple Southern feast.

PREP TIME: 15 minutes

COOKING TIME: 5–6 hours

ADDITIONAL STEPS: Pick over and wash the peas; soak the peas overnight in cold water

INGREDIENTS

- **1 pound (455 g) black-eyed peas**

- **½ pound (225 g) smoked ham hock**

- **1 medium-size onion**

- Salt and pepper to taste

Pick over the black-eyed peas, discarding discolored peas and any grit or stones. Put the rest of the peas into a bowl and cover with water 3 to 4 inches (7.5 to 10 cm) above the top of the peas. Soak overnight.

Drain the peas. Put the ham hock and the black-eyed peas into the slow cooker. Peel the onion and chop into small dice. Add the onion to the slow cooker with enough water to just cover the peas and season with salt and pepper to taste. Cook for 5 to 6 hours on low, until the water is almost gone and the peas are tender.

YIELD: *4 to 6 servings*

NUTRITIONAL ANALYSIS

361 calories; 8g fat (19.9% calories from fat); 26g protein; 47g carbohydrate; 8g dietary fiber; 40mg cholesterol; 36mg sodium.

✚ ADD IT IN!

Add a bay leaf to the recipe to heighten the play of flavors.

Cajun Red Beans and Rice

Here's a New Orleans staple, and it's good for you, too.

PREP TIME: 10 minutes
COOKING TIME: 2 hours on high or 4–5 hours on low

INGREDIENTS

- **2 cups (390 g) converted rice**

- **1 (14-ounce or 395-g) can small red beans**

- **1 tablespoon (6 g) Cajun spice mix**

- Salt and pepper to taste

Put the rice into the slow cooker. Drain the beans and add them to the rice. Add the Cajun spice mix and season with salt and pepper to taste. Add 3 ¹/₂ cups (825 ml) water. Stir to combine. Cook for 2 hours on high or 4 to 5 hours on low, until the water is absorbed and the rice is tender.

YIELD: *6 to 8 servings*

NUTRITIONAL ANALYSIS

177 calories; trace fat (1.1% calories from fat); 6g protein; 38g carbohydrate; 2g dietary fiber; 0mg cholesterol; 192mg sodium.

✚ ADD IT IN!

You can add more spice mixture or hot sauce to "kick it up." Just promise us you won't say "Bam!" when you do.

 Chili Beans

These are nice in a burrito or as a side with any Tex-Mex feast.

PREP TIME: 10 minutes

COOKING TIME: 1^1/$_2$ hours on high or 3–4 hours on low

INGREDIENTS

- **1 medium-size onion**

- **2 (16-ounce or 455-g) cans pinto beans**

- **3 or 4 ancho chiles or other favorite dried chile**

- Salt and pepper to taste

Peel the onion and chop into small dice. Add the onion to the slow cooker. Drain the beans and add them to the cooker. Remove the stems and seeds from the chiles and break them up into the slow cooker. Add ^{1}/$_2$ cup (120 ml) water, season with salt and pepper to taste, and stir. Cook for 1^1/$_2$ hours on high or 3 to 4 hours on low.

YIELD: *6 to 8 servings*

NUTRITIONAL ANALYSIS

103 calories; trace fat (3.6% calories from fat); 6g protein; 20g carbohydrate; 5g dietary fiber; 0mg cholesterol; 474mg sodium.

Gussied-Up Baked Beans

Give those canned baked beans some personality, and give this recipe your own twist by choosing your favorite barbecue sauce.

PREP TIME: 10 minutes

COOKING TIME: 1 hour on high or 3–4 hours on low

INGREDIENTS

- **2 (16-ounce or 455-g) cans baked beans**

- **1/2 cup (125 g) barbecue sauce**

- **1/4 cup (60 g) Dijon mustard**

Combine all the ingredients in the slow cooker. Cook for 1 hour on high or 3 to 4 hours on low.

YIELD: *8 to 10 servings*

NUTRITIONAL ANALYSIS

98 calories; 1g fat (7.3% calories from fat); 5g protein; 21 g carbohydrate; 5g dietary fiber; 0mg cholesterol; 537mg sodium.

Stewed Lentils with Red Wine

Because lentils are seldom used in mainstream American cuisine, this dish may be the road less taken for many people. But it's a fabulous side to lamb and beef. Try it and see for yourself!

PREP TIME: 15 minutes
COOKING TIME: 2 hours on high or 6–7 hours on low
ADDITIONAL STEPS: Wash and pick over the lentils

INGREDIENTS

- **1 pound (455 g) lentils**

- **1 medium-size onion**

- **2 cups (470 ml) red wine**

- Salt and pepper to taste

Pick over the lentils, removing any shriveled or discolored ones and any grit or stones, and rinse them in a colander. Put the lentils into the slow cooker.

Chop the onion into small dice and add to the slow cooker. Add the red wine and 1 cup (235 ml) water, and season with salt and pepper to taste. Cook for 2 hours on high or 6 to 7 hours on low, until the lentils are tender and the liquid is mostly absorbed.

YIELD: *4 to 6 servings*

NUTRITIONAL ANALYSIS

319 calories; 1g fat (2.4% calories from fat); 22g protein; 46g carbohydrate; 23g dietary fiber; 0mg cholesterol; 59mg sodium.

> **✚ ADD IT IN!**
>
> Finely chop a couple of carrots and mix them in when you add the onion.

CHAPTER 10
PASTA

S low cookers can do the casserole thing, too, with a few modi-
fications. Those homey baked pasta dishes so popular at
many dinner tables translate well to the slow cooker. From
Baked Ravioli (page 215) to Penne with Broccoli (page 221), these
pasta dishes can stand duty as either a hearty side dish or a main
meal by themselves. (Of course, many of the other recipes in this
book use pasta as an ingredient; check the index to find them. But in
the recipes in this chapter, pasta plays the starring role.)

 # Baked Ravioli

Here's a comforting classic that adapts to your favorite ravioli. Most stores stock frozen cheese and meat ravioli, both of which work fine here.

PREP TIME: 30 minutes
COOKING TIME: 1¹/₂ hours on high or 3–4 hours on low
ADDITIONAL STEPS: Precook the ravioli for 6 minutes

INGREDIENTS

- **1 pound (455 g) frozen ravioli**

- **1 (20-ounce or 570-ml) jar marinara sauce**

- **1 cup (115 g) shredded mozzarella cheese**

Bring a large pot of salted water to a boil. Add the ravioli and cook at a low boil for 6 minutes. Drain the pasta.

Spray the crock with nonstick cooking spray. Add the ravioli and the marinara sauce. Stir gently to combine well. Sprinkle the mozzarella on top. Cook for 1¹/₂ hours on high or 3 to 4 hours on low.

YIELD: *4 to 6 servings*

NUTRITIONAL ANALYSIS

250 calories; 12g fat (42.8% calories from fat); 12g protein; 24g carbohydrate; 2g dietary fiber; 95mg cholesterol; 916mg sodium.

 ADD IT IN!

Sprinkle fresh finely grated Parmesan cheese on top of the mozzarella before cooking for added zing.

 Baked Ziti

This is another of those comforting and homey casseroles that migrates well to slow-cooker land.

PREP TIME: 30 minutes
COOKING TIME: 1¹/₂ hours on high or 3–4 hours on low
ADDITIONAL STEPS: Precook the ziti for 8 minutes

INGREDIENTS

- **1 pound (455 g) ziti**

- **1 (20-ounce or 570-ml) jar four-cheese marinara sauce**

- **1 cup (260 g) basil pesto**

Bring a large pot of salted water to a boil. Add the ziti and cook at a low boil for 8 minutes. Drain the pasta and rinse with cold water to cool.

Spray the crock with nonstick cooking spray. Add the ziti and the marinara and pesto sauces. Stir to combine well. Cook for 1¹/₂ hours on high or 3 to 4 hours on low.

YIELD: *6 to 8 servings*

NUTRITIONAL ANALYSIS

403 calories; 16g fat (36.8% calories from fat); 13g protein; 50g carbohydrate; 3g dietary fiber; 9mg cholesterol; 502mg sodium.

✚ ADD IT IN!

You can add a top layer of grated Parmesan cheese to this dish if you like lots of cheese.

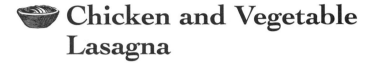 Chicken and Vegetable Lasagna

A white lasagna is an intriguing take on the traditional red sauce version, and it's just as delicious.

PREP TIME: 30 minutes
COOKING TIME: 3 hours on high or 6–7 hours on low
ADDITIONAL STEPS: Precook the lasagna for 8 minutes

INGREDIENTS

- 1 pound (455 g) dry lasagna pasta

- 2 (16-ounce or 485-ml) jars four-cheese Alfredo sauce

- 1 (16-ounce or 910-g) package frozen chicken and vegetable mix

Bring a large pot of salted water to a boil. Add the lasagna and cook at a low boil for 8 minutes. Drain the pasta and rinse with cold water to cool.

Spray the crock with nonstick cooking spray. Coat the bottom of the slow cooker with 1 cup (235 ml) Alfredo sauce, and then layer with lasagna. You may have to cut the pieces of lasagna to get them to fit into the round pot. Spread the pasta with one-fourth of the chicken and vegetables, and top with 1 cup (235 ml) Alfredo sauce. Repeat the layering process, finishing with Alfredo sauce. Cook for 3 hours on high or 6 to 7 hours on low. Allow to sit for 10 to 15 minutes before serving.

YIELD: *6 to 8 servings*

NUTRITIONAL ANALYSIS

492 calories; 24g fat (44.3% calories from fat); 17g protein; 52g carbohydrate; 2g dietary fiber; 83mg cholesterol; 635mg sodium.

Creamy Spinach Lasagna

This creamy, cheesy take on lasagna looks as good as it tastes.

PREP TIME: 30 minutes

COOKING TIME: 2 hours on high or 4–5 hours on low

ADDITIONAL STEPS: Precook the lasagna for 8 minutes; soften the creamed spinach

INGREDIENTS

- **1 pound (455 g) dry lasagna pasta**

- **2 (12-ounce or 340-g) packages frozen creamed spinach**

- **2 cups (160 g) shredded Parmesan cheese**

Bring a large pot of salted water to a boil. Add the lasagna and cook at a low boil for 8 minutes. Drain the pasta and rinse with cold water to cool. While the pasta is cooking, heat the spinach in a saucepan over medium heat until softened.

Spray the crock with nonstick cooking spray. Coat the bottom of the slow cooker with 1 cup (225 g) spinach, and then layer with lasagna. You may have to cut the pieces of lasagna to get them to fit into the round pot. Spread the pasta with more spinach, then sprinkle ¹/₂ cup (40 g) cheese over. Repeat the layering process, finishing with spinach and cheese. Cook for 2 hours on high or 4 to 5 hours on low. Allow to sit for 10 to 15 minutes before serving.

YIELD: *6 to 8 servings*

NUTRITIONAL ANALYSIS

408 calories; 15g fat (34.1% calories from fat); 17g protein; 49g carbohydrate; 3g dietary fiber; 25mg cholesterol; 571 mg sodium.

> **✚ ADD IT IN!**
>
> Dot the spinach layer with small spoonfuls of ricotta cheese.

 # Lasagna Casserole

Hungry for some classic lasagna with red sauce? Simple and satisfying anytime, lasagna is always a family favorite. Pair it with a salad and some crusty garlic bread, and you're in dinner heaven.

PREP TIME: 30 minutes
COOKING TIME: 2 hours on high or 4–5 hours on low
ADDITIONAL STEPS: Precook the lasagna for 8 minutes

INGREDIENTS

- **1 pound (455 g) dry lasagna pasta**

- **1 (32-ounce or 905-g) jar pasta sauce with meatballs**

- **4 cups (460 g) shredded mozzarella**

Bring a large pot of salted water to a boil. Add the lasagna and cook at a low boil for 8 minutes. Drain the pasta and rinse with cold water to cool.

Spray the crock with nonstick cooking spray. Coat the bottom of the slow cooker with pasta sauce, and then layer with lasagna. You may have to cut the pieces of lasagna to get them to fit into the round pot. Spread the pasta with more pasta sauce, then sprinkle 1 cup (115 g) cheese over the top. Repeat the layering process, finishing with sauce and cheese. Cook for 2 hours on high or 4 to 5 hours on low. Allow to sit for 10 to 15 minutes before serving.

YIELD: *6 to 8 servings*

NUTRITIONAL ANALYSIS

479 calories; 22g fat (42.6% calories from fat); 24g protein; 44g carbohydrate; 1g dietary fiber; 75mg cholesterol; 259mg sodium.

✚ ADD IT IN!

Shake some dried or chopped fresh oregano over each meat sauce layer, and dot a few spoonfuls of ricotta cheese on top as well.

🍜 Macaroni and Cheese Bake

Mom liked to add chunks of hot dog to this dish back in our childhood days, but we prefer to add ham these days.

PREP TIME: 30 minutes
COOKING TIME: $1^1/_2$ hours on high or 3–4 hours on low
ADDITIONAL STEPS: Precook the macaroni for 6 minutes

INGREDIENTS

- **1 pound (455 g) elbow macaroni**

- **1 (16-ounce or 475-ml) jar Alfredo sauce**

- **3 cups (345 g) shredded cheddar cheese, divided**

Bring a large pot of salted water to a boil. Add the macaroni and cook at a low boil for 6 minutes. Drain the pasta.

Spray the crock with nonstick cooking spray such. Add the macaroni, the Alfredo sauce, and 2 cups (230 g) cheese. Stir to combine well. Top with the remaining 1 cup (115 g) cheese. Cook for $1^1/_2$ hours on high or 3 to 4 hours on low.

YIELD: *6 to 8 servings*

NUTRITIONAL ANALYSIS

491 calories; 25g fat (45.9% calories from fat); 21 g protein; 46g carbohydrate; 1g dietary fiber; 76mg cholesterol; 569mg sodium.

> ### ✚ ADD IT IN!
>
> Stir in 1 cup (150 g) chopped, cooked ham and with Alfredo sauce and cheese.

 Penne with Broccoli

This creamy and delicious recipe works wonderfully as both a side and a main dish.

PREP TIME: 30 minutes
COOKING TIME: 1 hour on high or 3–4 hours on low
ADDITIONAL STEPS: Precook the penne for 8 minutes; add the penne and cheese after 45 minutes

INGREDIENTS

- **1 (16-ounce or 455-g) package frozen broccoli with cheese sauce**

- **1/2 pound (230 g) penne pasta**

- **1 cup (80 g) shredded Parmesan cheese**

Spray the crock with nonstick cooking spray. Put the frozen broccoli with cheese sauce into the slow cooker. Cook on high for 45 minutes. While the broccoli is cooking, bring a large pot of salted water to a boil. Add the penne and cook at a low boil for 8 minutes. Drain the pasta and add it to the slow cooker. Stir to combine the pasta and the broccoli and sauce, then top with the Parmesan cheese. Continue to cook on high for 1 hour or on low for 2 to 3 hours.

YIELD: *4 servings*

NUTRITIONAL ANALYSIS

362 calories; 8g fat (21.1 % calories from fat); 17g protein; 52g carbohydrate; 2g dietary fiber; 14mg cholesterol; 884mg sodium.

> **✚ ADD IT IN!**
>
> You can spice up this dish with a few shakes of red pepper flakes, or add a couple of cloves of minced garlic for a pungent kick.

Sausage and Pasta Bake

Gemelli is a good pasta to use for this hearty dish, but you can substitute other sturdy shapes, such as penne.

PREP TIME: 30 minutes
COOKING TIME: 1¹/₂ to 2 hours on high or 3–4 hours on low
ADDITIONAL STEPS: Precook the gemelli for 8 minutes

INGREDIENTS

- **1 pound (455 g) gemelli pasta**

- **1 (32-ounce or 905-g) jar marinara sauce with sausage chunks**

- **2 cups (500 g) ricotta cheese**

Bring a large pot of salted water to a boil. Add the gemelli and cook at a low boil for 8 minutes. Drain the pasta.

Spray the crock with nonstick cooking spray. Add the gemelli and the marinara sauce, along with the ricotta cheese. Stir to combine well. Cook for 1¹/₂ to 2 hours on high or 3 to 4 hours on low.

YIELD: *6 to 8 servings*

NUTRITIONAL ANALYSIS

484 calories; 22g fat (41.4% calories from fat); 19g protein; 52g carbohydrate; 3g dietary fiber; 50mg cholesterol; 595mg sodium.

✚ ADD IT IN!

Add 1 cup (115 g) shredded mozzarella cheese to the gemelli for more cheesy goodness. A handful of chopped fresh basil is also delicious.

🥣 Zesty Baked Bowties

Bowtie, or farfalle, pasta is a great pasta to bake, and the novel shape provides eating entertainment for the small-fry.

PREP TIME: 30 minutes
COOKING TIME: 1¹/₂ hours on high or 3–4 hours on low
ADDITIONAL STEPS: Precook the farfalle for 8 minutes

INGREDIENTS

- **1 pound (455 g) farfalle (bowtie) pasta**

- **1 (20-ounce or 570-ml) jar puttanesca sauce**

- **3 cups (345 g) shredded mozzarella, divided**

Bring a large pot of salted water to a boil. Add the farfalle and cook at a low boil for 6 minutes. Drain the pasta.

Spray the crock with nonstick cooking spray. Add the farfalle and the puttanesca sauce. Add 2 cups (230 g) mozzarella. Stir to combine well. Add ¹/₂ cup (115 ml) water. Top with the remaining 1 cup (115 g) cheese. Cook for 1¹/₂ hours on high or 3 to 4 hours on low.

YIELD: *6 to 8 servings*

NUTRITIONAL ANALYSIS

374 calories; 13g fat (30.4% calories from fat); 18g protein; 47g carbohydrate; 2g dietary fiber; 38mg cholesterol; 605mg sodium.

✚ ADD IT IN!

Olive lovers might want to stir even more chopped black olives into the casserole. (There are already some olives in the puttanesca sauce.)

Ziti with Creamy Sun-Dried Tomato Sauce

Sun-dried tomato pesto adds rich flavor to this dish. Pestos have proliferated in the marketplace and come in a variety of flavors and packages, from fresh to bottled. This recipe will adapt to fit many different flavors of pesto, so feel free to experiment.

PREP TIME: 30 minutes
COOKING TIME: 1¹/₂ hours on high or 3–4 hours on low
ADDITIONAL STEPS: Precook the ziti for 8 minutes

INGREDIENTS

- **1 pound (455 g) ziti**

- **1 cup (260 g) sun-dried tomato pesto**

- **1 (16-ounce or 475-ml) jar Alfredo sauce**

Bring a large pot of salted water to a boil. Add the ziti and cook at a low boil for 8 minutes. Drain the pasta.

Spray the crock with nonstick cooking spray. Add the ziti, pesto, and Alfredo sauce. Stir gently. Cook for 1¹/₂ to 2 hours on high or 3 to 4 hours on low.

YIELD: *6 to 8 servings*

NUTRITIONAL ANALYSIS

445 calories; 19g fat (38.6% calories from fat); 13g protein; 56g carbohydrate; 3g dietary fiber; 32mg cholesterol; 701 mg sodium.

✚ ADD IT IN!

Stir a handful of fresh chopped basil into the casserole before cooking. You can garnish each plate with more of the same for a visual exclamation point.

CHAPTER 11

DESSERTS

W hether you are a dedicated fan of end-of-meal deca-
dence in your own right or somebody who views
dessert only as a useful tool for getting your kids to eat
their vegetables, it's clear that the after-entrée entry is universally
popular. Although slow cookers don't spring immediately to mind as
dessert-making implements, a surprising number of recipes lend
themselves to this canny little appliance. From the homey warmth of
Blueberry Cobbler (page 226) to the dinner-party elegance of
Poached Pears in Red Wine (page 233), these recipes are guaranteed to please.

Blueberry Cobbler

Hot blueberry cobbler—yum! We specify yellow cake mix, but you can use spice cake, if you prefer.

PREP TIME: 15 minutes
COOKING TIME: 2 hours on high or 4–5 hours on low

INGREDIENTS

- **2 pints (580 g) fresh or frozen blueberries**
- **1 package (4 cups or 500 g) yellow cake mix, divided**
- **1 egg**
- **¹/₂ cup (120 ml) vegetable oil**

Put the blueberries into the slow cooker. Add ³/₄ cup (95 g) cake mix and stir. In a mixing bowl, combine the remaining 3¹/₄ cups (405 g) cake mix, the egg, the oil, and 1 cup (235 ml) water. Stir to make a smooth batter and pour it over the blueberries. Cook for 2 hours on high or 4 to 5 hours on low, until the cake is cooked through and the blueberries are bubbling.

YIELD: *6 to 8 servings*

NUTRITIONAL ANALYSIS

576 calories; 25g fat (39.0% calories from fat); 5g protein; 84g carbohydrate; 3g dietary fiber; 25mg cholesterol; 629mg sodium.

+ ADD IT IN!

Top with whipped cream or vanilla ice cream.

Chocolate Bread Pudding

Chocolate bread pudding is both decadent and cozy—all in all, it's a mouthwatering dessert. You can serve this hot or cold.

PREP TIME: 15 minutes
COOKING TIME: 4–5 hours

INGREDIENTS

- **5 or 6 chocolate muffins**

- **3 cups (705 ml) light cream**

- **3 eggs**

Cut the muffins into 2-inch (5-cm) cubes and put them into the slow cooker, pushing them in lightly to flatten. In a bowl, whisk together the cream and the eggs, then pour the mixture over the muffins. Press the muffin cubes down with a spoon so that they are all soaked in the egg mixture. Cook for 4 to 5 hours on low.

Serve hot or cold.

YIELD: *4 to 6 servings*

NUTRITIONAL ANALYSIS

525 calories; 37g fat (62.4% calories from fat); 11g protein; 40g carbohydrate; 3g dietary fiber; 195mg cholesterol; 343mg sodium.

✚ ADD IT IN!

Top this yummy offering with whipped cream and a handful of fresh raspberries.

Chocolate Fondue

We have suggested angel food cake to dip into the fondue, but if you want to convince yourself that dessert is a healthy course, this is also delicious served with a variety of fruits, such as strawberries, kiwi, pineapple, and pears.

PREP TIME: 15 minutes

COOKING TIME: 2 hours

INGREDIENTS

- **1 pound (455 g) good-quality semisweet chocolate (bar or chips)**

- **1 cup (235 ml) half-and-half**

- **1 store-bought angel food cake**

If the chocolate is a solid piece, cut it into small pieces and put it into the slow cooker. If you use chips, just put them into the cooker. Pour the half-and-half over the chocolate and cook for 2 hours on low. Stir until the mixture is smooth. Cut the cake into cubes and dip it into the fondue.

Note: You can make this ahead and hold it on warm for an extended period while serving.

YIELD: *6 to 8 servings*

NUTRITIONAL ANALYSIS

502 calories; 21 g fat (34.2% calories from fat); 8g protein; 81 g carbohydrate; trace dietary fiber; 11 mg cholesterol; 398mg sodium.

Cinnamon Eggnog Bread Pudding

Smooth, creamy, and soothing, a good bread pudding is a fine ending to any meal. You can serve this one hot or cold.

PREP TIME: 15 minutes
COOKING TIME: 4–5 hours on low

INGREDIENTS

- **1 (1-pound or 455-g) loaf cinnamon swirl bread**

- **3 cups (705 ml) eggnog**

- **3 eggs**

Cut the bread into 2-inch (5-cm) cubes and put them into the slow cooker, pushing them in lightly to flatten. In a bowl, whisk together the eggnog and the eggs, then pour the mixture over the bread. Press the bread down with a spoon so that it is all soaked in the egg mixture. Cook for 4 to 5 hours on low.

Serve hot or cold.

YIELD: *4 to 6 servings*

NUTRITIONAL ANALYSIS

477 calories; 22g fat (40.6% calories from fat); 12g protein; 60g carbohydrate; 0g dietary fiber; 168mg cholesterol; 733mg sodium.

Granola Apple Crisp

Slow cookers are not known for their browning and crisping abilities, but by using granola as our topping, we can build that quality in, and the result is a great dessert. It is a bit more on the chewy side than an oven-baked crisp, but we love it anyway.

PREP TIME: 30 minutes
COOKING TIME: 2–3 hours on high or 4–5 hours on low

INGREDIENTS

- **3 pounds (1365 g) apples, such as Granny Smith**

- **1 cup (200 g) sugar**

- **2 cups (300 g) granola**

Peel and core the apples. Cut the apples into wedges and put them into a large bowl. In a small bowl, stir together the sugar and cinnamon together and toss with the apples. Put the mixture into the slow cooker. Top with the granola and cook on high for 2 to 3 hours or on low for 4 to 5 hours, until the apples are soft and bubbling.

YIELD: *6 to 8 servings*

NUTRITIONAL ANALYSIS

340 calories; 9g fat (22.1% calories from fat); 4g protein; 66g carbohydrate; 8g dietary fiber; 0mg cholesterol; 4mg sodium.

✚ ADD IT IN!

We generally consider vanilla ice cream *de rigueur* as an accompaniment to any crisp.

Layered Crêpe Dessert

This rich dessert features the classic flavor combination of raspberries and chocolate.

PREP TIME: 15 minutes
COOKING TIME: 4–5 hours

INGREDIENTS

- **20 premade dessert crêpes**
- **4 cups (700 g) good-quality semisweet chocolate chips**
- **4 cups (440 g) red raspberries**

Spray the crock with nonstick cooking spray. Arrange 4 crêpes to cover the bottom of the cooker and top with 1 cup (175 g) chocolate and 1 cup (110 g) raspberries. Repeat the layers, ending with crêpes. Cook for 4 to 5 hours on low, then turn off the slow cooker and allow the dessert to sit for 30 minutes. Cut into wedges.

YIELD: *6 to 8 servings*

NUTRITIONAL ANALYSIS

559 calories; 32g fat (46.8% calories from fat); 8g protein; 74g carbohydrate; 10g dietary fiber; 62mg cholesterol; 79mg sodium.

✚ ADD IT IN!

A whipped cream topping would be perfect, or add a dollop of crème fraîche if you want to gussy it up a little.

Peaches with Dumplings

This is a great dessert on those summer days when the peaches are at their ripest.

PREP TIME: 30 minutes
COOKING TIME: 2 hours

INGREDIENTS

- **3 pounds (1365 g) peaches**

- **1³/₄ cups (350 g) sugar, divided**

- **2 cups (250 g) self-rising flour**

- ³/₄ cup (170 g) shortening, such as Crisco

Bring a large pot of water to a boil and drop the peaches in for 30 seconds. Drain and run under cold water to cool. Peel the peaches and cut the flesh from the pits (stones) and into wedges. Put the peaches into the slow cooker and add 1 cup (200 g) sugar. Stir to combine.

In a mixing bowl, combine the flour and the remaining ³/₄ cup (150 g) sugar. Stir. Add the shortening and cut it into the dry ingredients with a pastry cutter, two knives, or your fingers. Stir 1 cup (235 ml) water into the dry ingredients just enough to make a batter.

Drop the batter by spoonfuls onto the peaches in the slow cooker. Cook for 2 hours on high, until the biscuit batter is cooked through and the peaches are bubbling.

YIELD: *4 to 6 servings*

NUTRITIONAL ANALYSIS

600 calories; 26g fat (38.6% calories from fat); 4g protein; 89g carbohydrate; 1g dietary fiber; 0mg cholesterol; 530mg sodium.

✚ ADD IT IN!

Adding 1 teaspoon (2.2 g) nutmeg or 2 teaspoons (4.6 g) cinnamon to the peaches makes a nice spice accent. Feel free to serve with ice cream or whipped cream.

Poached Pears in Red Wine

This dish is simple and elegant as a stand-alone dessert, or you can use these pears in tarts or napoleons.

PREP TIME: 30 minutes
COOKING TIME: 4 hours

INGREDIENTS

- **6 pears**

- **2 cups (400 g) sugar**

- **4 cups (940 ml) red wine**

Peel the pears, leaving the stems intact. Put the pears into the slow cooker. In a small bowl, combine the sugar and wine. Add to the slow cooker. Cook on low for 4 hours, until the pears are soft but not mushy. Remove the pears from the poaching liquid. You may serve them warm or cold. The poaching liquid can be reduced to make a syrup to go with the pears; simply boil it over high heat until it thickens.

YIELD: *6 servings*

NUTRITIONAL ANALYSIS

475 calories; 1g fat (1.7% calories from fat); 1g protein; 96g carbohydrate; 5g dietary fiber; 0mg cholesterol; 104mg sodium.

✚ ADD IT IN!

Add 2 tablespoons (14 g) ground cinnamon to the sugar-wine mixture for added flavor.

Warm Applesauce

This homey favorite is terrific served over ice cream or pound cake.

PREP TIME: 20 minutes
COOKING TIME: 4–6 hours

INGREDIENTS

- **6 large cooking apples, such as Cortland**

- **³/₄ cup (150 g) sugar**

- **1 tablespoon (7 g) apple pie spice, or more to taste**

Peel and core the apples, then cut them into small chunks. Put the apples, sugar, and spice into the slow cooker and add ¹/₄ cup (60 ml) water, stirring to combine. Cover and cook on low for 4 to 6 hours.

YIELD: *6 servings*

NUTRITIONAL ANALYSIS

181 calories; 1g fat (2.4% calories from fat); trace protein; 47g carbohydrate; 4g dietary fiber; 0mg cholesterol; 1mg sodium.

Homey Baked Apples

We like the tartness that dried cranberries bring to the mix, but you can substitute any of your favorite dried fruits here.

PREP TIME: 20 minutes
COOKING TIME: 3–5 hours

INGREDIENTS

- **6 large cooking apples, such as Cortland**

- **1 $^{1}/_{2}$ (180 g) cups dried cranberries**

- **1 cup (340 g) maple syrup**

Core the apples and put them upright in the slow cooker. Pour $^{1}/_{2}$ cup (120 ml) water into the bottom of the cooker. Fill the center of each apple with the dried cranberries, and drizzle the maple syrup over the apples. Cook on low for 3 to 5 hours, until the apples are soft but not mushy.

YIELD: *6 servings*

NUTRITIONAL ANALYSIS

220 calories; 1g fat (2.3% calories from fat); trace protein; 57g carbohydrate; 4g dietary fiber; 0mg cholesterol; 5mg sodium.

CHAPTER 12

BEVERAGES

E verybody loves the warmth of mulled cider or rich cocoa when wintertime arrives, and a slow cooker is an excellent choice for heating beverages. Its gentle, slow heat warms milk-based drinks without scalding them, and it keeps beverages warm indefinitely—no fuss, no muss, and no pitchers, warming trays, and other paraphernalia to worry about. So ladle up a cup of your favorite beverage and draw up a seat. These drinks will soothe your soul and quench your thirst.

 # Chai Tea

Chai tea is the drink du jour, *and with good reason. Simultaneously spicy and rich, this delicious tea can become addictive!*

PREP TIME: 10 minutes
COOKING TIME: 1 hour

INGREDIENTS

- **2 cups (470 ml) chai tea concentrate**

- **4 cups (940 ml) milk**

- **2 teaspoons (4.6 g) cinnamon**

Put the chai concentrate and milk into the slow cooker and stir together. Cook on high for 1 hour, until the liquid is steaming. You may turn the cooker to low if you are holding the tea for a party. Sprinkle the top of each serving with a little cinnamon.

YIELD: *4 to 6 servings*

NUTRITIONAL ANALYSIS

131 calories; 5g fat (36.8% calories from fat); 7g protein; 14g carbohydrate; 1g dietary fiber; 22mg cholesterol; 94mg sodium.

 ADD IT IN!

Stir in ¼ cup (85 g) orange honey to sweeten the chai.

Raspberry Iced Tea

Yes, this is an iced tea recipe made in a slow cooker. You will need to make this ahead so that you have time to chill the beverage before serving.

PREP TIME: 10 minutes
COOKING TIME: 1¹/₂ hours
ADDITIONAL STEPS: Strain and chill the tea after cooking

INGREDIENTS

- **8 black tea bags, or 1 cup (115 g) loose black tea**

- **2 cups (500 g) frozen raspberries, plus some fresh ones for garnish**

- **1 cup (200 g) sugar**

Put the tea, raspberries, sugar, and 8 cups (1880 ml) water into the slow cooker. Stir. Cook for 1¹/₂ hours on high. Strain the tea, pushing down on the solids in the strainer. Discard the tea and raspberries. Chill the brewed tea. Serve over ice with additional raspberries for garnish.

YIELD: *6 to 8 servings*

NUTRITIONAL ANALYSIS

166 calories; trace fat (0.5% calories from fat); 1g protein; 43g carbohydrate; 3g dietary fiber; 0mg cholesterol; 4mg sodium. Exchanges: 1 fruit; 1¹/₂ other carbohydrates.

Rich Hot Chocolate

Homemade cocoa is immeasurably tastier than the powdered mixes. Top this with some marshmallow crème or whipped cream for a decadent treat.

PREP TIME: 10 minutes
COOKING TIME: 1¹/₂ hours on high
ADDITIONAL STEPS: Add the milk after the chocolate is melted

INGREDIENTS

- **4 ounces (115 g) unsweetened chocolate**

- **1 cup (200 g) sugar**

- **6 cups (1410 ml) milk**

Put the chocolate and sugar into the slow cooker. Cook for about ¹/₂ hour on low, until the chocolate is melted. Stir the chocolate and sugar together, then whisk in the milk in a stream. Turn the heat to high and cook for another 45 minutes to 1 hour, until the milk is steaming.

YIELD: *4 to 6 servings*

NUTRITIONAL ANALYSIS

378 calories; 19 g fat (41.1% calories from fat); 10 g protein; 50 g carbohydrate; 3 g dietary fiber; 33 mg cholesterol; 123 mg sodium.

✚ ADD IT IN!

Sprinkle some cinnamon into the mix for an added zing.

Scandinavian Spiced Hot Lemonade

Also known as grains of paradise, cardamom is a very popular spice in Scandinavian cooking. This lemonade is good for when you have a cold, or when you are just cold.

PREP TIME: 20 minutes
COOKING TIME: 1¹/₂ hours on high or 3–4 hours on low
ADDITIONAL STEPS: Squeeze and strain the lemons

INGREDIENTS

- **10 to 12 lemons**

- **1¹/₂ cups (510 g) honey**

- **10 to 12 whole cardamom pods**

Squeeze the lemons and strain the juice to make 1¹/₂ cups (355 ml) lemon juice. Put the lemon juice into the slow cooker. Add 8 cups (1880 ml) water and the honey. Stir. Add the cardamom pods. Cook on high for 1¹/₂ hours or on low for 3 to 4 hours.

YIELD: *8 to 10 servings*

NUTRITIONAL ANALYSIS

One serving of the basic recipe contains 00 calories; 00 g fat; 00 g protein; 00 g carbohydrate; 00 g dietary fiber; 00 mg cholesterol; 000 mg sodium.

 Spiced Mulled Cider

This is perfect for warming up on a chilly fall afternoon or for serving at your neighborhood Christmas party. Be sure to use cider, not apple juice—it's not the same otherwise! The texture and taste of apple juice are very different from those of cider, which has a more complex flavor.

PREP TIME: 10 minutes
COOKING TIME: 1^1/$_2$ hours on high or 3–4 hours on low

INGREDIENTS

- ^{1}/$_2$ **gallon (1.9 litres) apple cider**
- **4 whole cinnamon sticks**
- **8 to 10 whole cloves**

Pour the cider into the slow cooker and add the cinnamon sticks and cloves. Cook on high for 1^1/$_2$ hours or on low for 3 to 4 hours.

YIELD: *6 to 8 servings*

NUTRITIONAL ANALYSIS

One serving of the basic recipe contains 00 calories; 00 g fat; 00 g protein; 00 g carbohydrate; 00 g dietary fiber; 00 mg cholesterol; 000 mg sodium.

 ADD IT IN!

Stir in ^{1}/$_2$ teaspoon (1.1 g) nutmeg.

INDEX

ACKNOWLEGMENTS

As always, cookbooks don't get written by the authors alone—we depend on a network of families, friends, and colleagues to provide a heaping measure of support, patience, advice, and feedback. And we are very grateful for this help.

Our families provided plenty of help and humor. We'd like to thank Don, Sarah, Olivia, Nicholas, Erica, and Sam for heroically sitting through an unending array of slow cooker offerings. Our parents, George and Marge Hildebrand, were, as always, in the thick of the fray, as were our siblings and their lovely spouses: Amy and Darrell; and Charles and Jerrie. Thank you!

The slow cooker enthusiast community is many and varied, and we had help from a number of very kind folks who put their slow cookers and dinner menus in our hands, as it were.

Thanks to Betty Obernesser, Jean Bruns, and many of the members of the West Boxford Second Congregational Church Ladies Charitable Society for help with recipe testing.

Finally, thanks to the members of Whimsicality, particularly Ed Wohlford and his family, for more recipe testing and general support. You guys are all peachy.

ABOUT THE AUTHORS

Robert Hildebrand is the executive chef at Three Stallions Inn in Randolph, Vermont. His work has been featured in *Bon Appetit,* as well as several newspapers.

Carol Hildebrand is an award-winning writer and editor. Her work has appeared in *Boston Magazine, The Old Farmer's Almanac, CIO, Darwin,* and many others.

They are the co-authors of *500 3-Ingredient Recipes* and *500 5-Ingredient Desserts.*